3–
10/22

HOW TO SPEND $75 BILLION
TO MAKE THE WORLD
A BETTER PLACE

HOW TO SPEND
$75 BILLION
TO MAKE THE WORLD
A BETTER PLACE

Edited by

Bjørn Lomborg

COPENHAGEN
CONSENSUS
CENTER

This book was published by the Copenhagen Consensus Center.

www.copenhagenconsensus.com

Permission queries can be emailed to *info@copenhagenconsensus.com*

Second Edition Copyright ©2014 by Copenhagen Consensus Center
Cover design by Vivien Rostási
Printed in Canada by Victoria Bindery

ISBN 978-1-940003-03-0

CONTENTS

Dear reader,

This book contains lots of smart ideas on how to solve the world's challenges. It is based on evidence and estimates from the world's top economists. Because of the nature of the book and its format, you might find yourself skipping around. And that's fine. The book isn't necessarily meant to be read consecutively. Feel free to start with the topics that intrigue you the most. If you want to dive in deeper, you can also read excerpts from the actual research papers in the appendix.

I hope you will use this to take a stand, and set your own global priorities for how to make the world a better place. And share your ranking on *www.RankSmartSolutions.com*.

all the best,

bjorn

Introduction

By Bjørn Lomborg

YOU HAVE $75 BILLION
TO SAVE THE WORLD

How would you spend it?

If you had $75 billion to spend over the next four years and your goal was to advance human welfare, especially in the developing world, how could you get the most value for your money?

That is the question that I posed to a panel of five top economists, including four Nobel Laureates, in the Copenhagen Consensus 2012 project. The panel members were chosen for their expertise in prioritization and their ability to use economic principles to compare policy choices.

Over the past year, more than 50 economists prepared research on nearly 40 investment proposals to address problems ranging from armed conflicts and natural disasters to hunger, education, and global warming. The teams that drafted each paper identified the costs and benefits of the smartest ways to spend money within their area. In early May 2012, many of them traveled to Denmark to convince the expert panel of the power of their investment proposals.

While they met in Copenhagen, I presented readers of Slate magazine with the same proposals. In polls accompanying each article, I asked Slate readers to basically answer the same question as the Nobel Laureates: How would you prioritize these investments to best help the world? We compiled the Slate readers' votes, and this book includes their ranking (p.57) to show how it differs from the Nobel Laureate results.

The expert panel's findings reveal that, if spent smartly, $75 billion— just a 15 percent increase in current aid spending—could go a long way to solving many of the world's challenges.

Given the budget constraints, they found 16 investments worthy of investment (in descending order of desirability):

1. Bundled interventions to reduce undernutrition in preschoolers (to fight hunger and improve education)

2. Expanding the subsidy for malaria combination treatment
3. Expanded childhood immunization coverage
4. Deworming of schoolchildren, to improve educational and health outcomes
5. Expanding tuberculosis treatment
6. R&D to increase yield enhancements, to decrease hunger, fight biodiversity destruction, and lessen the effects of climate change
7. Investing in effective early warning systems to protect populations against natural disaster
8. Strengthening surgical capacity
9. Hepatitis B immunization
10. Using low-cost drugs in the case of acute heart attacks in poorer nations (these are already available in developed countries)
11. Salt reduction campaign to reduce chronic disease
12. Geoengineering R&D into the feasibility of solar radiation management
13. Conditional Cash Transfers for School Attendance
14. Accelerated HIV Vaccine R&D
15. Extended field trial of information campaigns on the benefits of schooling
16. Borehole and public hand-pump intervention

The single most important investment, according to the panel, would be to step up the fight against malnutrition. As I reported in the Slate series, new research for the project by John Hoddinott and colleagues of the International Food Policy Research Institute and Peter Orazem of Iowa State University focuses on an investment of $3 billion annually. This would purchase a bundle of interventions, including micronutrient provision, complementary foods, treatment for worms and diarrheal diseases, and behavior-change programs, all of which could reduce chronic undernutrition by 36 percent in developing countries.

In total, such an investment would help more than 100 million children start their lives without stunted growth or malnourishment. And comprehensive research now shows that such interventions would stay with them for life: Their bodies and muscles would grow faster, their cognitive abilities would improve, and they would pay more attention in school (and stay there longer). Studies show that, decades down the line, these children would be more productive, make more money, have fewer kids, and begin a virtuous circle of dramatic development.

Such opportunities come sharply into focus when you ask some of the world's best minds to find the biggest bang for the buck. Micronutrient provision is rarely celebrated, but it makes a world of difference.

Likewise, just $300 million would prevent the deaths of 300,000 children if it were used to strengthen the Global Fund's malaria-financing mechanism, which makes combination therapies cheaper for poor countries. Put in economic terms, the benefits are 35 times higher than the costs—even without taking into account that it safeguards our most effective malaria drug from future drug resistance.

For a similar amount, 300 million children could be dewormed in schools. By not sharing their food with intestinal parasites, they, too, would become more alert, stay in school longer, and grow up to be more productive adults—another cause that needs much more public attention.

Expanding tuberculosis treatment and childhood immunization coverage are two other health investments that the expert panel endorses. Likewise, a $100 million annual increase in spending to develop a vaccine against HIV/AIDS would generate substantial benefits in the future.

As people in the developing world live longer, they are increasingly experiencing chronic disease; indeed, half of all deaths this year will be from chronic diseases in Third World countries. Here, the panel finds that spending just $122 million could achieve complete Hepatitis B vaccine coverage and avert about 150,000 annual deaths from the disease. Getting low-cost drugs for acute heart attacks to developing countries would cost just $200 million and prevent 300,000 deaths.

The expert panel's findings point to a compelling need to invest roughly $2 billion annually in research and development to increase agricultural output. Not only would this reduce hunger by increasing food production and lowering food prices; it would also protect biodiversity, because higher crop productivity would mean less deforestation. That, in turn, would help in the fight against climate change as well, because forests store carbon.

When it comes to the issue of climate change, the experts recommend spending a small amount—roughly $1 billion—to investigate the feasibility of cooling the planet through geoengineering options. This would allow us to understand better the technology's risks, costs, and benefits. Moreover, the research could potentially give us low-cost, effective insurance against global warming.

Another priority for investment is the establishment of effective early-warning systems for natural disasters in developing countries. For less than $1 billion a year, this would alleviate both direct and long-term economic damage, possibly securing some $35 billion in benefits.

The $75 billion budget chosen for the Copenhagen Consensus project is large enough to make a real difference, but small enough that we must choose—as in the real world—the projects that can achieve the most good. The expert panel's list shows us that there are many smart solutions waiting to be implemented.

But we would like to leave the question open to the readers as well. What's your view? Are these investments that you think that policymakers and philanthropists should prioritize? We have set up the website *www.RankSmartSolutions.com* so that you can weigh in and share your own prioritized list.

ABOUT THE
COPENHAGEN CONSENSUS
APPROACH

The Copenhagen Consensus approach is to look at global issues and to ask: how could economic science help us to improve decision-making?

Each day decisions are made about global political priorities. Governments, philanthropists, and international bodies choose to support some worthy causes while others are disregarded. Unfortunately, these decisions frequently do not take fully into account a comprehensive economic view of the effects, benefits, and costs of solving one problem instead of another.

The conflicting demands of the media, stakeholders, and politicians mean that priorities are set in an obfuscated environment.

The idea behind Copenhagen Consensus is to render this process less arbitrary, and to provide more evidence upon which informed decisions can be made by politicians and others. We create a framework in which solutions to the world's biggest problems are prioritized explicitly, with the goal of achieving the most 'good' for people and the planet.

Much of the time, society is presented with a menu of choices, but with very little information on their costs and benefits. The Copenhagen Consensus process aims to put prices and sizes on the menu, making choice easier and more informed. To inform this process in practice, we ask: if you were to spend an additional $75 billion over the next four years to do good for humanity and the environment, where would you spend it first?

This book constitutes a concrete contribution designed to improve the debate regarding global priorities: the questions of how we tackle the world's problems, where we start, and what should sensibly be done.

This section sets out the methodological approach to the Copenhagen Consensus 2012 project and adumbrates the research that follows.

Past Projects

In 2004 and 2008, the Copenhagen Consensus Center gathered research on ten key global challenges – from malnutrition to terrorism – and commissioned a panel of expert economists to rank the investments. The research from Copenhagen Consensus 2004 and Copenhagen Consensus 2008 is available in Cambridge University Press books, 'Global Crises, Global Solutions' and 'Global Crises, Global Solutions: Second Edition' (Cambridge University Press, 1st edn., 2005, 2nd edn., 2009).

These projects attracted attention from all around the world. Denmark's government spent millions more on HIV/AIDS projects, which topped the economists' 'to do' list in 2004. Micronutrient delivery programs in Africa and elsewhere received significant attention and greater resources after they topped the list in 2008. The World Bank quoted Copenhagen Consensus research and findings in 2006 when it created its new strategy on combatting malnutrition: "As documented by the Copenhagen Consensus, we know what to do to improve nutrition and the expected rates of returns from investing in nutrition are high."

In 2006, Copenhagen Consensus United Nations brought together 24 United Nations ambassadors, including the Chinese, Indian and American ambassadors, and set them the task of prioritizing limited resources along Copenhagen Consensus lines to improve efforts to mitigate the negative consequences of global challenges.

Consulta de San José in 2007 (the Copenhagen Consensus for Latin America and the Caribbean) was a collaboration with the Inter-American Development Bank. This project gathered highly esteemed economists to identify the projects that would best improve welfare in Latin America and the Caribbean. The research is available as 'Latin American Development Priorities' (Cambridge University Press, 2009).

In 2009, the approach was applied to climate change. The Copenhagen Consensus on Climate assembled an Expert panel of five world-class economists, including three recipients of the Nobel Prize, to evaluate 21 research papers on different responses to climate change and to deliberate on which solutions would be most effective; this project was published in 'Smart Solutions to Climate Change' (Cambridge University Press, 2009).

In 2011, RethinkHIV – funded by the Rush Foundation – saw the Copenhagen Consensus Center gather teams of economists and medical scientists to perform the first comprehensive, cost/benefit analysis of HIV/AIDS investment opportunities in sub-Saharan Africa. This research was published in 2012 as 'RethinkHIV' (Cambridge University Press, 2012).

These projects generated considerable attention and discussion. They showed that an informed ranking of solutions to the world's big problems is possible, and that cost/benefit analyses—much maligned by some—lead to a compassionate, clear focus on the most effective ways to respond to the real problems of the world's most afflicted people.

Copenhagen Consensus 2012

How to Spend $75 Billion to Make the World a Better Place builds on several of these past projects – particularly Copenhagen Consensus 2004 and Copenhagen Consensus 2008 – which each gathered expert panels of outstanding economists to deliver ranked lists of the most promising solutions to ten of the most pressing challenges facing the world. Each project involved around 60 leading economists and specialists in ten global challenges.

This effort also draws on the research for the Copenhagen Consensus on Climate and RethinkHIV, to ensure that the most up-to-date and informed analysis is provided for the topics of global warming and HIV/AIDS.

The objective for Copenhagen Consensus 2012 was to commission new research and data to deliver an informed, current perspective on the smartest investments to respond to global challenges.

Tremendous progress has been made in the fight against humanity's biggest ailments within our lifetimes. People in most countries live longer, healthier lives; air and water quality in the developed world is generally getting better; and a much larger proportion of the global population is being adequately fed.

But there are still many problems to tackle. The minority of us lucky enough to have been born in the developed world can sometimes take for granted universal education, an assured food supply and clean, piped water. But billions of people are not so lucky. And although the world's problems fall disproportionately on the developing world, rich countries also face problems.

When it comes to global welfare projects, it is easy for decision-makers to pay lip service to prioritization, while behaving as though the pool of money is infinite, that all that is lacking is willpower, and that everything should be tackled all at once.

Many of the big decisions are made individually by the governments of donor countries, or by relatively specialist international agencies that receive money from rich nations and use it for the benefit of the world, especially developing countries. Each such organization has its own remit, scope of work, and funding base.

Of course, in principle we ought to deal with all of the world's woes. We should win the war against hunger, end conflicts, stop communicable diseases, provide clean drinking water, step up education and halt climate change. But we cannot do all of this at once. We live in a world with limited resources and even more limited attention for our biggest problems. This means we have to ask the crucial question: if we can't do it all, what should we do first?

This book focuses on the funding that the developed world spends on improving the world in general. Of course, most nations spend the vast bulk of their resources on themselves – perhaps 99 percent of developed nations' GDP. In a well-functioning political system, this internal system is prioritized according to a solid framework of economic principles, as well as by social and ethical concerns.

However, the last one percent of spending – the portion that goes outside a nation's borders – is less well developed. This spending ranges from the money that goes from donor nations as Official Development Assistance (ODA) to spending on peacekeeping forces, research into vaccines, and efforts to reduce environmental pollution.

Often, explicit prioritization is ignored altogether by policymakers. The United Nations Millennium Development Goals (MDGs), which shaped much of this funding for the first decade of this century, consist of a laundry list of noble causes with no consideration given to relative costs or benefits.

Methodology

The Copenhagen Consensus approach aims to inform global debates by giving an overview of economic research and facts with given global problems. The identification of costs and benefits for different interventions, allows prioritization to be based on economic evidence. Relying on costs and benefits, as this project does, is a transparent and practical way to establish whether spending is worthwhile or not. It lets us avoid the fear and media hype that often dictate the way that we see the world. Carefully examining where an investment would have the biggest rewards provides a principled basis upon which important decisions can be made. Assigning a monetary value is the best way we have of introducing a common frame for comparison.

Some will argue that it is impossible to put a value on a human life. Yet, refusing to put a value on human life does not help to save lives. In practice, prioritization occurs every day in areas as disparate as health policy and infrastructure. When we decide on a national speed limit we are implicitly putting a price on human life, weighing the benefits of fewer lives lost with a lower speed limit against the dispersed costs of higher transport times. Making such tradeoffs explicit allows us all to better evaluate our choices. In this book, we use tools such as the 'Disability Adjusted Life Year' (DALY) which allows economists – and thus, policymakers – to add up the years of life that are lost and establish the impact of disability, and then weigh these with other benefits and costs of different policies. Specifically, we have set low and high values of DALY at $1,000 and $5,000 to ensure comparability across areas.

Another economic tool that informs this project is discounting, which allows us to balance our own needs against those of future generations, and ensure that we have a consistent approach across all of the challenges presented in the book. So, what discount rate have we used, and why?

Commercial projects typically discount at the rate of current or expected market interest rates. Economists often recommend a rate of 6 percent for discounting development projects, and we have suggested this as a baseline for the economists who wrote research for this project.

9

However, some argue that humanity should take a longer view and set a lower discount rate. Hence, we have also asked authors to use a rate of 3 percent for comparison. Such an approach makes virtually all projects look more attractive but especially those (like education or global warming) which take longer to produce significant benefits. Which rate is more appropriate is something we leave up to the individual experts – and you as a reader – but crucially, it is important to have a consistent discount rate across all areas.

Using these economic tools, we can then gauge how the relative benefits and costs change as we alter discount rates, the value of DALYs, or change our assumptions about the relative likelihood of outcomes. Such results make the prioritization of different policies much more transparent.

2012 Challenges

The challenges chosen for the first Copenhagen Consensus exercise in 2004 were drawn from a larger list of areas that receive the attention of United Nations organizations and winnowed down by the suggestions from the expert panel. Likewise, for Copenhagen Consensus 2012, we asked the panel of Nobel Laureates and economists to provide us with input on the challenges with the most promising solutions, so that the 2012 list is fully updated.

Ideally the project would make a full examination of all possible challenges, but in a world of limited resources, with the help four Nobel Laureates, we identified the ten top challenges, ensuring a wide coverage of the most important issues of the time. Compartmentalizing all issues within these ten challenges is of course an approximation. This means we can ask a team of expert economists to address the individual area, examine the available literature, and make a proper cost/benefit analysis. However, in reality, boundaries are not clearly defined. Action in one area will often have indirect positive or negative effects in others.

As you will see in this book, authors and the Expert Panel have taken such effects into account as much as possible. The aim of a Copenhagen Consensus Challenge Paper is to present empirically based cost/benefit analysis studies of the highest academic standards within each challenge. These are the central source for the Copenhagen Consensus expert panel whose considerations can be found in the 'Expert Panel Ranking' section of this book. Two more papers are provided as well, which are called 'Alternative Perspectives'. The purpose of these is to balance the Challenge Papers and to indicate important issues that were not sufficiently dealt with in the Challenge Paper. The Alternative Perspectives are short, reviewing published research that might have been left out of the original challenge paper, and providing alternate interpretations on the estimates or other strengths, weaknesses and omissions in the economic models. Their role is primarily to spur discussion and reveal substantial professional differences regarding the subject.

Throughout all the analysis we have asked authors to use a comparable economic framework. If each of the challenge papers is in the same 'language', then decision-makers – and you, the reader – will be able to establish what can be achieved with spending in different areas. In the following section "Smart Solutions to Global Challenges," you will find reviews of all of the research submitted on the top ten chosen topic areas.

Ranking

In the section on 'Ranking the Opportunities', a panel of five economists – including four Nobel Laureates – provides their views of the solutions. Economists were chosen – as in the past – because they are experts in prioritization and comparing costs and benefits across the many different challenges.

As in the previous Copenhagen Consensus projects, this group – comprising Thomas Schelling, Nancy Stokey, Finn Kydland, Vernon Smith, and Robert Mundell – examined all of the research presented here. They traveled to Copenhagen and engaged with all of the core authors over three days. Each session started with a short presentation by the Challenge Paper author, and then these authors were interviewed by the panel. The specialists then left, and the experts discussed their considerations and reasons for ranking the solutions before they ended the session.

The experts each came to their own conclusions about the merits of each suggested solution to each challenge. As in past Copenhagen Consensus exercises, their consensus findings were achieved by taking the median of the expert rankings as the ranking in the common list (found in the 'Final Prioritized Ranking'). This procedure provided a common ranking while ensuring that if one expert changed his or her ranking at the extreme, this would not make the general ranking change, but would rather require a majority of experts to change their ranking.

In the section on 'Ranking the Opportunities', you will find not only the economists' consensus, and shared opinion, but also their individual rankings. Their work highlights some of the most cost-effective responses to global challenges.

It is vital, however, that these important issues are not just left to economists. This book serves to give everybody the opportunity to consider (and reconsider) their own priorities. The framework presented here provides a way for you to compare investments side-by-side. Which do you find we should focus on first? Which would help the world the most? Which deserve more attention from policy-makers in your region? And, crucially, what are you going to do about it?

Smart Solutions to Global Challenges

By Bjørn Lomborg

EDUCATION

To Educate Children, We Have To Teach Their Parents

We can improve education in poor countries by showing parents the importance of schooling.

Over the past 50 years, remarkable progress has been made ensuring that children receive basic education. More than 60 percent of adults in low-income countries can read and write, whereas in 1962, just one-third were literate. Today, nearly nine in 10 children around the world complete primary school.

However, in education—as in other developmental challenges—progress is uneven. Across sub-Saharan Africa, nearly one-quarter of primary aged children are not in school. In Equatorial Guinea, 46 percent of children are not being educated. In South Asia, progress has generally been impressive, but 34 percent of Pakistan's primary aged children are not in school. The worst educational outcomes occur in the nations that rank among the most poorly governed.

In a research paper on education Peter Orazem highlights the different ways that decision-makers could approach the challenge of providing education in developing countries.

Most children in developing countries are now already enrolled in school for at least some period, so Orazem points out that we could focus on strategies that improve school quality, either by enhancing the learning that is occurring in school or increasing the number of years of schooling.

Unfortunately, there is very weak knowledge about which inputs actually generate quality schooling outcomes, and many investments are unlikely to generate the desired effects. There is widespread acknowledgement that resources are used inefficiently, but for instance efforts to

15

improve resource management by devolving authority to local jurisdictions are as likely to fail as succeed.

Thus, Orazem considers three strategies that seem to offer the best evidence of success to date: nutrition supplements, offering information on returns to schooling, and conditional cash transfers for school attendance. All have been shown to succeed with benefits that exceed the costs.

It may seem surprising to focus on nutrition to achieve better schooling, but malnourished children learn poorly. Ensuring proper nutrition when brain development is occurring makes a significant difference. The benefits are not just educational but also increase health and a child's physical abilities (investment in deworming is recommended in the Copenhagen Consensus research on chronic disease, and nutritional interventions are promoted in the paper on hunger.) Provision of nutrient supplements and anti-parasitic medicines is very inexpensive: In Kenya the cost of deworming a child can be as low as $3.50, with benefits 20 to 50 times higher.

Increasing the years a child spends in school simply by providing accurate information to kids and parents on the returns of education is another promising and relatively inexpensive intervention.

Many kids and parents, especially in rural areas, are simply unaware of the long-term benefits that may come from a better education. In Madagascar, for instance, providing children and their parents with accurate information on the value of schooling has been achieved at a cost of $2.30 per child, resulting in total benefits of possibly 600 times the cost.

Although the costs vary across countries, such an intervention could conceivably be built into the standard curriculum at relatively low cost and has the potential of increasing academic effort while in school as well as increasing years of schooling. However, because of very few studies, the benefits from a large-scale information campaign are less certain.

Finally, Orazem argues that the most consistent evidence of success in recent years comes from making payments to underprivileged parents conditional on their children attending school.

These programs—known as conditional cash transfers—have consistently increased child attendance, even when the transfer is modest. Administrative costs have been lower than those of other social interventions. In addition to positive schooling outcomes, these transfers have lowered the poverty rate, improved the nutritional status of poor households, and have increased the proportion of children receiving vaccinations and other health services. While there is great variance in performance, a dollar spent on such programs on average produces benefits of about $9.

Because the programs increase the intensity of child investment in school as well as child time in school, they help to break the cycle of poverty whereby poor parents underinvest in their children's schooling and doom their children to poverty.

By increasing child attendance, Orazem argues, we should even see an increase in teacher attendance, which will increase the quality of schooling offered to the poorest children.

Yet, cash transfer programs are much more expensive than nutrition or health interventions. That might explain why cash transfer programs are concentrated in wealthier countries while nutrition programs typically focus on the poorest countries.

In general, the climate for all of these interventions is worse where the positive returns are depressed by poor government institutions. Therefore, the best places to try these interventions are countries that protect individual economic and political freedoms. Of course, those countries would also have the better capacity to implement an intervention, whether distributing medication, transfer payments, or information on the benefits of investing in schooling.

ARMED CONFLICT

War Is a Long, Messy Hell

And it's more important than ever that we try to prevent it in the first place.

Without peace and stability, there are impediments to solving every other challenge that we look at in the Copenhagen Consensus 2012 series. Armed conflict is a major global problem that disproportionately affects the world's poorest. Not a single low-income country afflicted by violence has achieved even one of the eight Millennium Development goals.

In each year of the 1980s and 1990s there were between 30 and 40 major armed conflicts in progress, though over the past decade, major armed conflicts have declined. In 2007, there were 14 major armed conflicts in 13 locations around the world, nearly all of which were civil wars. There was a wide variation in the intensity of these conflicts, from "low intensity" battles between guerrillas and governments, to conflicts between relatively large and well-equipped armies.

There are now more states than ever and also more disputes, but still relatively few of these lead to war. Though there are now fewer fights, they last longer than they once did. The types of conflicts range from the ideological struggles that we see in Mozambique, Eritrea, or Nicaragua, to the more fragmented decentralized conflicts such as those of Somalia and Rwanda. Many are a mixture of both.

The nature of war has changed with a decreasing role for formal armies, lack of battlefield engagement, and increased victimization of civilians.

The costs from conflicts can be immense and devastating—yet they are almost always understated because we ignore the legacies that violence leaves behind. The immediately apparent, direct costs are obviously loss of life and injury on the battlefield. But in many countries, conflict leads to far greater casualties because of economic collapse so that fewer can afford health care, proper food, and education. Because of the long lag in economic recovery after a conflict, people will die for years after a conflict ends. In addition to the direct and legacy costs, there are spinoff costs such as the expense of looking after refugees displaced by one country's internal strife.

In a research paper for Copenhagen Consensus 2012, Paul Dunne attempts to tally all of these costs and work out the benefits of using more and new funds to respond to armed conflicts in different ways.

Clearly, the complex nature of conflict makes finding solutions immensely challenging. To be able to approach the problem more easily, Dunne focused on the three obvious points at which we can try to reduce the devastating impact of conflict: preventing it in the first place, intervening to end it when it occurs, and helping to reconstruct a post-conflict area.

According to Dunne's analysis, conflict prevention is the most cost-effective solution. The causes of conflict are hugely varied and the roots of war are multifaceted, with important historical contexts. There are a number of factors that can be identified including colonial legacy, military governments and militaristic cultures, ethnicity and religion, unequal development, inequality and poverty, bad leadership, polity frailties and inadequacies, external influences, greed, and natural resources.

So how can we stop conflicts before they occur? Dunne pinpoints early warning mechanisms, peacekeeping operations, economic sanctions, and aid as the tools that have proved effective.

Dunne calculates that spending about $56 billion over four years on a combination of these measures would lead to benefits on the magnitude of at least $606 billion. Among these benefits, the avoided deaths, injuries, and other conflict-related violence are perhaps the most compelling arguments for the use of available funds for prevention.

Given the high possible benefits of avoided carnage and relatively low costs, conflict prevention has a benefit/cost ratio of at least 11. This means that, when we frame it in economic terms so that it can be compared to other interventions, each dollar spent achieves benefits worth at least $11.

If conflicts do break out, the next stage is intervention. At this stage it will be impossible to avoid a significant part of the cost of conflict, and the intervention itself will also be more costly. The projected $100 billion cost of intervention includes better intelligence, economic sanctions, and aid, as well as likely military intervention. This is nearly double the cost of preventing a conflict in the first place. Yet, with benefits of at least $606 billion, there are still large pay-offs. For each dollar spent, we can avoid conflict damage worth about $5, making intervention a cost-effective use of resources.

When conflicts end, what is needed for reconstruction is contingent on the nature of the conflict and the way that it ended. Most of the costs of conflict have already been incurred, but experience shows it is possible to speed recovery and reduce the risk of relapse into further violence. Particularly important are the legacy costs of the conflict, such as more general violence within the society. Post-conflict policies can be costly but are also cost-effective in preventing suffering and building up societies and economies that provide new markets and raw materials. According to research by former Copenhagen Consensus expert panel member and researcher Paul Collier, economic reconstruction reduces the risk of a renewed outbreak of conflict by 42 percent in 10 years.

The cost of post-conflict policies is higher than intervention at around $140 billion, and the benefits are also smaller at $404 billion. In total, it is estimated that each dollar will avoid at least $3 of conflict damage. While post-conflict policies may not have the highest benefit/cost ratio, Dunne argues that they are crucial in ensuring successful development can occur. For that reason, these policies are already attracting considerable resources from the international donor community.

Dunne emphasizes that although he has examined many of the different ways that conflicts impose a cost on society, the true cost is still likely to be hugely underestimated. There are immeasurable quantities and legacy costs that are difficult to identify. The existence of drugs, criminal gangs, and violence in South American countries such as Colombia in the present day, for example, can be traced back to the ending of an armed conflict without true peace being achieved.

Too often, developed and stable nations have turned a blind eye to conflicts, and have done too little, too late. This analysis shows that, at the very least, from an economics perspective, there are sound reasons to change that approach.

CLIMATE CHANGE

Can You Really Make Clouds Whiter and More Reflective?

Scientists are getting there, and it might be the one of the best ways to fight climate change.

Of all of the issues in the Copenhagen Consensus 2012 project, climate change is perhaps the most discussed and emotional. Although efforts to strike an international climate deal have come to naught, more newspaper space and celebrity attention has been devoted to this issue in the past decade than any other.

Copenhagen Consensus 2012 devotes four research papers to this topic. These papers build on a 2009 Copenhagen Consensus project that focused solely on this topic. (You can read all of the project's research in this Cambridge University Press book, *Smart Solutions to Climate Change*.) This lets us look at very different ways to deal with this global challenge.

Let's look first at the path that policymakers have chosen so far. Richard Tol makes the case that there is wide agreement in the economic literature that reducing greenhouse gas emissions is best done through a carbon tax. Climate policy, he notes, is not about spending money. It is about raising money (and, of course, about finding the best way to spend the revenues raised through a carbon tax).

Tol argues that the costs of deep emission cuts are relatively small if the following conditions are met: emission reduction targets are lenient at first but accelerate over time; every part of the economy emitting carbon is regulated; all gases are regulated and at the same price; all countries reduce emissions; and climate policy is coordinated with other policies. If these rules are violated, then the costs of reducing harmful emissions rapidly escalate.

Unfortunately, policymakers violate these rules a lot in the real world. It is increasingly clear that governments have great difficulty in delivering the cheapest possible emission-reduction programs. (See Tol's earlier paper looking at the very large price tag of European Union climate change policies.)

Very stringent emission-reduction targets such as the long-term goals of the European Union simply do not pass the benefit/cost test: They actually cause more damage than they prevent. However, very modest reductions in carbon emissions appear to be justifiable with any number of assumptions, while more stringent emission reduction needs more favorable assumptions.

Tol finds that a low tax of about $1.80 on each ton of carbon would generate benefits (of avoided climate damage) worth between $1.50 and $9. However, a high tax set at $250 would cost much more than it would gain, with benefits of just two cents to 12 cents, putting it in the category of *"does more damage than it prevents."*

Isabel Galiana and Christopher Green propose a technology-led climate policy. This means dramatically increased research and development, testing and demonstration of scalable, reliable, and cost-effective low carbon emitting energy technologies. This will be funded by a low but gradually rising carbon tax, but unlike Tol's proposal the main focus is on innovating cheap, green energy sources.

They argue that the size of the energy technology challenge is huge, and there is a current lack of technological readiness and scalability in low-carbon energy sources. They show that adopting a "brute force" approach to reducing emissions with a carbon tax before green technology is actually ready to take over from fossil fuels could generate economic costs 10 times or more than widely published estimates of CO_2 mitigation cost estimates.

The authors argue that while the importance of new technologies to slowing and eventually reducing global emissions is more widely accepted than it once was, there have been no fundamental developments on the low-carbon energy front in recent years. Moreover, funding has gone mainly to subsidizing manufacture and deployment rather than to research. With continued increases in carbon emissions despite an enduring global economic crisis, the case for a technology-led climate policy is stronger than ever.

Galiana and Green conclude that increased funding for low-carbon research and development would have benefits ranging from three to 11 times higher than the cost, depending on the rate of success and time horizon.

But what can we achieve by preparing ourselves for climate damage? Carlo Carraro, Francesco Bosello, and Enrica De Cian look at what can be achieved with adaptation policies.

They find that the most important impacts of global warming will be on agriculture and tourism, where nations will lose, on average, about one-half of one percent of GDP from each by mid-century. However, they point out that much of this damage will actually be avoided by people choosing for themselves to adapt to the change in their environment. Farmers will choose plants that thrive in the heat. New houses will be designed to deal with warmer temperatures.

Taking this into account, rich countries will adapt to the negative impacts of global warming and exploit the positive changes, actually creating a total positive effect of global warming worth about one-half a percentage point of GDP.

However, poor countries will be hit harder. Adaptation will reduce the climate-change-related losses from 5 percent of GDP to slightly less than 3 percent, but this is still a significant negative impact. The real challenge of global warming, therefore, lies in tackling its impact on developing nations. Here, more needs to be done, above and beyond the adaptation that will happen naturally.

Adaptation may serve multiple purposes, including helping developing countries to boost education, health, and economic development.

The researchers find that, broadly, every dollar spent on adaptation would achieve at least about $1.65 worth of positive changes for the planet.

The final paper, by J. Eric Bickel and Lee Lane, looks at geo-engineering. This essentially means cooling the planet by reflecting more of the sun's rays back to space. There are a few different ways to achieve this. One promising approach is stratospheric aerosol injection—where a precursor of sulfur dioxide would be continuously injected into the stratosphere, forming a thin layer of aerosols to reflect sunlight. The amount of sulfur required to offset global warming is on the order of 2 percent of the sulfur that humans already inject into the atmosphere, largely through burning fossil fuels. Another suggested approach is marine cloud whitening, where seawater would be mixed into the atmosphere at sea to make the clouds slightly whiter and more reflective.

Bickel and Lane do not suggest actually implementing such programs at this point, but they look at the costs and benefits of preparing the knowledge of how they might be deployed in the future. They estimate that the cost of a climate-engineering research and development program is on the order of $1 billion: a small fraction of what the United States alone is spending on climate-change research each year. They estimate that each dollar spent could create roughly $1,000 of benefits in economic terms.

Such high benefits reflect the fact that solar radiation management holds the potential of reducing the economic damages caused by both warming and costly CO_2 reduction measures (such as carbon taxes). These early-reduction costs tend to be higher than those of climate change; so by lessening the stringency of controls, climate-engineering may also provide near-term benefits—compared to strategies relying solely on emissions reductions.

Moreover, if climate change should suddenly get much worse (reaching the so-called "tipping points"), geoengineering appears to be the only technology that could quickly cool the Earth. This feature would allow it to act as an insurance against extreme and highly uncertain climate outcomes.

The four papers reveal four different paths to resolving the challenge of climate change.

BIODIVERSITY

We Still Need To Save the Rain Forests

Biodiversity efforts are often targeted toward saving cute animals. But the real problem is disappearing forests, wetlands, and mangroves.

We turn now to the problem of keeping resources available for future generations.

The issue of disappearing biodiversity has increasingly received mainstream media attention in the past few years and is starting to compete with climate change as the environmental threat that we talk about the most. Often, biodiversity campaigners have attempted to capture our attention with pictures of cuddly endangered animals or alarming figures about the rate of disappearing species.

In practice it is difficult to actually quantify the loss of biodiversity, let alone put a value on it. What scientists can do instead is measure "ecosystem services." These are the natural processes by which the environment produces resources used by humans, such as clean water, timber, habitat for fisheries, and pollination of native and agricultural plants. Also included are genetic materials that can help make new life-saving drugs, the recreational and cultural uses of natural environments, the control of agricultural pests, and the value of biomass storing CO_2 (as a counter to global warming).

The links between biodiversity and ecosystem services is still undergoing research. But the most important known fact is that these services have faced major (and measurable) losses. According to the Millennium Ecosystem Assessment, the planet during the last century lost 50 percent of its wetlands, 40 percent of its forests and 35 percent of its mangroves. About 60 percent of global ecosystem services have been degraded in just 50 years.

In a research paper on biodiversity for Copenhagen Consensus 2012, Salman Hussain and Anil Markandya find that there will be a significant loss of biodiversity over the next 40 years. They estimate that this loss could be about 12 percent globally, with South Asia facing a loss of 30 percent and sub-Saharan Africa 18 percent. They look at three interventions and compare these to doing nothing.

The first solution focuses on increasing agricultural productivity through research and development. This may seem like a roundabout way to address biodiversity, but as the global population has increased to 7 billion, we have cut down more and more forest to grow our food. Between now and 2050, we will likely expand agricultural areas another 10 percent, and that land will come from forests and grasslands. Thus, if we could increase agricultural productivity, we would need to take less and be able to leave more to nature. (It's interesting to note that investment in agricultural R&D is also suggested as a way of reducing hunger and malnutrition.)

The authors estimate that with a $14.5 billion annual infusion into research, we can achieve 20 percent higher annual growth rates for crops and 40 percent higher growth rates for livestock, which over the next 40 years will significantly reduce the pressure on nature.

Looking just at tropical forests, this would save an area the same size as Spain, along with a similar amount of temperate forests and more than twice that area of grasslands. In total, the benefits will be on the order of $53 billion. When we take into account that these forests will store more carbon, for every dollar spent, we will do about seven times the amount of good both for biodiversity and climate. And, of course, we will have made more food available and at cheaper prices for future generations, substantially increasing the total benefits.

Hussain and Markandya note that currently about 10 percent of all land globally is deemed to be "protected" from destruction. They explore increasing protected land to about 20 percent globally (across a large number of ecological regions), over three decades. There are obvious benefits but also significant costs, principally the loss of output from the land that is taken out of use.

Land scarcity arising from such a policy would likely force an increase in agricultural productivity. The cost estimates for the newly protected lands have a big impact on the overall results. With higher assumptions, the program costs more than it achieves, even when the benefits of avoided climate change are included. With lower assumptions it only barely passes, making $1 spent achieve slightly more than $1 worth of good.

However, Hussain and Markandya note that the main reason for this program would be to enhance biodiversity conservation; our current methods of estimation do not fully capture those benefits, so these estimates could be an underestimation.

Forests are one of the main sources of biodiversity. The final program Hussain and Markandya propose seeks to prevent all dense forests from being converted to agriculture over a 30-year period. The academics do not attempt to assess the political viability of such an approach. To use the same measure as above, it would save more than seven times the area of Spain in tropical forests.

The benefits are very high, but there is considerable uncertainty about the costs. With estimates they find reasonable, the benefits exceed the costs even without including the CO_2 storage value, and the solution is attractive because it will get a minimum of $7 back on the dollar.

The research laid out by Hussain and Markandya points to a range of concrete options we could take, if we're serious about responding to this challenge.

NATURAL DISASTERS

An Ounce of Prevention ...

It's harder for poor countries to respond to natural disasters. We should help them be better prepared before hurricanes and earthquakes strike.

Hurricane Katrina, Australian floods, Japan's 2011 earthquake and tsunami: Even the wealthiest, best-prepared countries can experience large-scale damage and destruction when natural disasters strike.

But the situation is much worse in poor countries without the resources to protect their population or economy against catastrophes. Building codes are lacking or poorly enforced, and infrastructure is insufficient to send out information before a disaster, or assist victims promptly after it hits. The 2010 earthquake in Haiti starkly illustrated what happens when natural disasters strike an unprepared and poor country.

Often poor countries only make the pages of our newspapers when disaster strikes. Tragic images prompt us to give generously to assist those who have been hurt or made homeless. But what if we adopted an "ambulance at the top of the cliff" approach and tried to increase the resiliency of developing countries to natural disaster?

Hurricanes, earthquakes, and floods impose an economic toll that can disrupt and undermine a fragile country for a long time. This cost is growing. According to the reinsurer Munich Re, direct economic losses from natural catastrophes amounted to $1.6 trillion from 2001 to 2011. Small island economies like St. Lucia and Samoa have suffered high losses to productivity because of disasters. Nature can impose a roadblock to the growth that lifts people out of poverty.

Costs from natural disasters are increasing largely because more people choose to live in harm's way. This trend, combined with the expectation of some events becoming more extreme because of changes in climate patterns, challenges the human capacity to adapt. In an innovative paper for Copenhagen Consensus 2012 written by Professors Howard Kunreuther and Erwann Michel-Kerjan propose a series of concrete actions that would reduce the vulnerability of poor nations to such large-scale catastrophes.

They propose investments in four risk-reduction measures. The first three proposals are designed to better protect against damage and loss of life from earthquakes, floods, and hurricanes, and the final one is intended to more generally increase the resilience of communities.

First, the authors propose designing schools that can withstand earthquakes to reduce damage and also the number of fatalities to children, teachers and other staff. Retrofitting the schools in all 35 most-exposed countries around the world would save the lives of 250,000 individuals over the next 50 years. Costs vary dramatically from country to country: In the Solomon Islands it would cost just $36 million to retrofit schools with cumulative total benefits worth $187 million, but for all other countries the benefits are dramatically lower, meaning that any program of global reach would probably pay back less than the initial investment.

Kunreuther and Michel-Kerjan's second proposal is to invest in community flood walls and elevated homes to protect areas subject to floods. It would cost $5.2 trillion to elevate by one meter all houses subject to flooding in the 34 countries most susceptible to this hazard and another $940 billion to build walls around the relevant communities in all 34 countries. The most cost-effective approach would be to invest $75 billion into building flood walls around some of these communities. Kunreuther and Michel-Kerjan calculate the benefits over the next 50 years as $4.5 trillion, making the benefits a remarkable 60 times higher than the costs. Those benefits would mostly come from reduction in damages, though the walls would also save 20,000 lives.

Thirdly, they propose strengthening the roofs of houses in countries with high exposure to hurricanes and cyclones to reduce losses from wind damage. This would cost $951 billion in the 34 countries most prone to high wind events, with benefits ranging between two and three times this amount. This measure would save 65,700 lives over the next 50 years.

Finally, Kunreuther and Michel-Kerjan explore setting up early disaster warning systems. Based on existing studies and research from Stephane Hallegatte, they find that early warning systems in developing countries would require less than $1 billion a year and would have direct benefits (reductions in the losses from disasters) of between $1 billion and $5.5 billion per year. There are additional benefits, such as the reduction in evacuation costs, the reduced costs to the health care system, improved continuity of education (from preserving schools), reduced social stress, and avoided business interruption, which is worth at least another $3 billion and possibly $30 billion. In total, the benefits could range from four to 35 times their cost.

But who should pay for disaster protection measures? As Kunreuther and Michel-Kerjan point out, there is a need to persuade international donors to start investing more systematically in disaster risk reduction before a disaster strikes, rather than focusing almost exclusively on post-disaster assistance, as they do today. Similarly, NGOs must put their time and energy into promoting measures that reduce future losses and fatalities rather than focusing on emergency relief. And more governments in developed countries and multinational corporations need to provide funding and technical expertise to assist low-income countries in undertaking these measures.

Kunreuther and Michel-Kerjan point out that the way that we often approach decisions, with short-term costs in mind rather than long-term benefits, can get in the way of policy-makers making the change in approach that they need to. To address these issues, they propose new programs such as multi-year insurance coupled and disaster-risk reduction loan programs, as well as alternative risk transfer instruments for covering catastrophic losses.

A disaster in one part of the world can have ripple effects on many other countries, so it should be in everybody's interest to try to increase resiliency. If a few key decision makers, organizations and countries take the initiative, this may lead others to follow suit, tipping the world in the right direction.

But the clock is ticking: Another large-scale disaster can happen tomorrow.

POPULATION GROWTH

The Thorny Issue of Population Growth

Life expectancy is up and poverty is down worldwide, even with our rapidly expanding global population. Are our fears of catastrophe overblown?

The world population is now over 7 billion. It added the last billion in merely 12 years, similar to the time it took to add the fifth and sixth billion. Despite this rapid growth, the doomsday predictions of previous decades about the potentially disastrous consequences of rapid population growth have not materialized. Indeed, during the recent decades of rapid global population growth, various summary measures of individual well-being have in fact increased: For example, from 1960 to 2010, global life expectancy increased from 51.2 to 67.9 years, infant and maternal death rates declined substantially, education—and, importantly, also levels of female schooling—increased, global per capita food production and consumption rose, and the proportion of the global population living in poverty declined significantly.

In the research for Copenhagen Consensus 2012, Hans-Peter Kohler of the University of Pennsylvania looks at sub-Saharan African nations that, among high-fertility countries, make the dominant contribution to world population growth. These nations are among the poorest and most vulnerable in the world, often having weak institutions and capacities to manage population growth.

"High-fertility" countries today account for about 38 percent of the 78 million people that are added annually to the world population, despite the fact that they are home to only 18 percent of the population. After 2060, the world's population is projected to grow exclusively as a result of population growth in today's high-fertility countries.

Kohler notes that the overall Sub-Saharan African population increase peaked in the early 1980s and has been declining from its pinnacle of 2.8

percent from the years 1980–85 to 2.5 percent in the years 2005–10, although growth remains more than twice as high as the global rate.

The overall growth rate masks substantial variation. Nine countries are expected to more than triple their population between 2010 and 2060, with population growth rates between 2.2 and 3.0 percent: Burkina Faso, Niger, Zambia, Malawi, Somalia, Tanzania, Uganda, Mali, and Madagascar.

Many high-fertility Sub-Saharan African countries have a considerable—and possibly growing—"unmet need" for family planning: This means women who are not using any contraception but do not want more children, or want to delay the next child. About 25 percent of sexually active women would like to limit their fertility but do not use family-planning methods.

Family-planning programs that facilitate a decline in fertility and a reduction in the population growth rate would seem to be potentially highly beneficial interventions that should be expanded. And yet, as Kohler outlines, this conclusion has been subject to a long-standing and sometimes heated debate, often questioning the very basic pillars of this deduction.

This debate has sometimes raised more questions than answers: How detrimental, if at all, is population growth for economic development, individual well-being, and the attainment of development indicators such as the Millennium Development Goals? Do family-planning programs have causal effects toward reducing fertility, or would observed declines in fertility areas also have been observed in the absence of these programs? Is there a window of opportunity in coming decades in which declines in population growth could provide a "demographic dividend" that would facilitate the social and economic development in some of the world's most developed countries?

In the last two decades, a growing body of research has substantially strengthened the case for family-planning programs—documenting, for example, the significant effects of these programs toward reducing fertility, increasing education for mothers, improving women's general health and longer-term survival, increasing female labor force participation and earnings, as well as child health.

However, the attempt to obtain reasonably reliable estimates of both the benefits and costs of these programs remains very challenging.

Kohler draws on recent estimates to find that expanding family-planning services to all women with unmet needs—215 million women—would require an additional annual expenditure of $3.6 billion, bringing the total annual cost to $6.7 billion. Three-quarters of these additional expenses would be required for program and other systems costs related to expanding family planning services, while only 16 percent would be required for the supplies and contraceptive commodities.

The benefits are large. Reduced fertility, increased child spacing, and possible reductions in unwanted fertility are likely to reduce infant and maternal mortality, each year leading to 150,000 fewer maternal deaths and 600,000 fewer motherless children. These effects alone, Kohler estimates, are worth more than $110 billion, meaning that each dollar spent will achieve $30 to $50 of benefits.

But moreover, it is also estimated that reduced fertility will lead to higher levels of female education, increases in female labor force participation and earnings. At the same time, fewer children and more men and women in the work force will increase economic growth over the coming decades. Essentially, reductions in fertility and population growth rates would result in sustained increases in GDP per capita over several decades. This could lead to an extra benefit of perhaps $60 for every dollar spent.

With the caveat that knowledge about the interactions between population and development remains limited and heated discussion takes place about many assumptions, Kohler's research suggests substantial benefit/cost ratios for family planning programs. Altogether, he finds that every dollar spent in this area could result in benefits worth about $90 to $150.

Kohler's analysis adds further weight to the argument that family planning programs are a good economic investment, especially in light of continued population growth in the world's worst-off countries: That upwards of one-quarter of women want to limit their fertility but are not using any contraception points to a real need for greater emphasis on this area.

WATER AND SANITATION

Developing the Smartphone of Toilets

More than 2.5 billion lack basic sanitation. We can fix that.

The story of water and sanitation is one of success and failure. The world has met the Millennium Development Goal on the provision of clean drinking water five years early, but is set to miss its goal on basic sanitation by almost one billion people. An astonishing one-third of the world population, 2.5 billion people, lacks access to basic sanitation. More than one billion people must defecate out in the open rather than using the toilets that we take for granted in the developed world.

Inadequate sanitation is much more than an inconvenience. It costs lives. It caused a cholera outbreak in Haiti in late 2010 that has now made 500,000 people sick and killed 7,000. Smaller cholera outbreaks are still commonplace during the rainy season in Bangladesh and the low-lying parts of many African cities. Diarrheal diseases are still a leading cause of death for children under 5, second only to respiratory infections. The World Bank concludes that the economic impact of poor sanitation can be as high as 7 percent of GDP for some Asian countries and close to 1 to 2 percent of GDP for African countries.

Copenhagen Consensus 2012 asked Frank Rijsberman and Alix Peterson Zwane from the Gates Foundation to establish the best ways to reduce the size of this challenge.

They found that development agencies overemphasize safe-water projects and underinvest in sanitation. Rijsberman and Zwane look at what it would cost to improve sanitation services for both the unserved population in developing countries (those one billion or so who must defecate in the open), and what it would cost to improve the quality of service for those people in urban areas who are nominally "served" but are confronted with the challenges of emptying and safely disposing of latrine or septic tank contents.

An estimated 200 million latrines and septic tanks are emptied manually, by a worker descending into the pit with a bucket and spade, and subsequently dumped or buried in the immediate environment, often reintroducing pathogens previously contained in the pit or tank.

They propose three solutions as potentially worthy of large-scale investment.

The first of these is Community Led Total Sanitation, the name given to various forms of an approach that emphasizes behavior change, particularly making it the community's responsibility to share in the creation of communities that are free from open defecation, particularly in rural areas. Rijsberman and Zwane base their calculations on a large-scale behavior-change program, reaching 23 million with a one-off delivery cost of $3 to $5 per person affected.

Given the rapid adoption of community-led total sanitation programs aiding tens of millions of people over the last 10 years and the relatively high rate of success in achieving "open-defecation free" communities, they consider this to be a comparatively low-risk intervention.

Their analysis implies that about 50 percent of people in rural areas—about 600 million people— who lack access to basic sanitation could be reached with a total investment of $3 billion, providing welfare benefits that are four to seven times higher.

The second intervention they explore is Sanitation as a Business. For the existing 2 billion latrines and septic tanks in developing countries, a critical bottleneck—one that affects the urban poor particularly—is that there are no affordable and sustainable services to effectively and efficiently empty them and process the fecal sludge safely and economically.

Typically, the sludge is just deposited on the ground, negating almost all of the health benefits of sanitation. The solution is to generate innovation in sanitation services, reducing the cost of this service from between $35 and $91 per household to just $10 per household per year. That cost pays for emptying the latrine or septic tank, transporting the fecal sludge to a treatment plant, and treating it to acceptable levels before reuse or dispersal into the environment. While speculative, the authors provide illustrative calculations that suggest that an investment in innovation to develop these technologies, including an initial subsidized rollout, would provide benefits to about 40 million people at a cost of $320 million and overall benefits worth between 27 and 46 times higher than the costs.

Third, Rijsberman and Zwane propose The Reinvented Toilet—one of the signature ideas of the Bill & Melinda Gates Foundation: efforts to stimulate technical innovation, particularly harnessing advances in physics, chemistry, and engineering, to create a radically reinvented toilet that recycles human waste into reusable products at the household scale.

Early in 2011, the Bill & Melinda Gates Foundation challenged more than 20 top universities to use modern science and engineering to come up with a significantly different form of processing and recycling human waste that does not depend on the sewer networks and large volumes of water for transportation. The challenge was to develop a system that is off the grid, affordable for the poorest members in society (meaning that it costs less than a nickel a day), and an aspirational product—something that everyone will want to use and that over time replaces the flush toilet as the new gold standard.

The foundation has awarded eight Reinvent the Toilet Challenge grants and funded another 57 small grants in 2011 that aim to innovate all or part of the non-sewered value chain. All complete reinvented toilets are currently at the laboratory/proof-of-concept to prototype stage and therefore investments in the development of this solution are high risk.

Assuming that this investment would lead to 100 percent coverage for all latrines currently emptied manually, this $125 million investment would pay back $40 for each invested dollar, serving one billion people. In addition, if successful, the Reinvented Toilet would serve many more of the other 3.5 billion people who currently don't have access to a flush toilet. Presuming a reinvented toilet can be successfully developed, and can become an aspirational product—the smartphone of sanitation—the issues of high cost, slow adoption, and limited benefits that variously plague the current generation of sanitation technologies will be overcome.

Rijsberman and Zwane's proposals are novel. But if we are to make the same gains in sanitation delivery as we have in water (and in other areas of developmental spending), then we need to get creative as well as make this area a higher priority.

INFECTIOUS DISEASES

Malaria Is Making a Comeback

But making sure new drugs are affordable for poor countries is still a cheap way to save hundreds of thousands of children.

It is difficult to overstate how much the fight against infectious disease has improved the human condition in the last century. In research written for Copenhagen Consensus 2012, economists Dean Jamison, Prabhat Jha, Ramanan Laxminarayan, and Toby Ord point out that improved immunization saves more lives per year than would be saved by global peace. The same is true for smallpox eradication, diarrhea treatment, and malaria treatment. Nonetheless major problems remain, and Jamison's team explores the ways to step up our battle against the biggest killer diseases, and identify five top priorities.

The most important of these is malaria treatment. The malaria parasite has developed a resistance to the effective, inexpensive, and widely available drugs that have previously provided an important partial check on the high levels of malaria child deaths in Africa.

The resistance to these older drugs is leading to a rise in deaths and illness that could number in the hundreds of thousands. A high priority for additional spending is to reduce the relative prices that poor countries face for new artemisinin combination therapies (through the so-called "Affordable Medicines Facility-malaria"). Every $1 million spent on this financing mechanism of the Global Fund means about 300,000 more children treated, including 20,000 with severe malaria. This would prevent 1,000 deaths. Thus, spending $300 million a year would prevent 300,000 child deaths, with benefits, put in economic terms, that are 35 times higher than the costs. Various donors are reviewing extending this Facility this fall, and this analysis suggests it is one of the best returns on health that could be made globally.

The second intervention is the control of tuberculosis, which kills more adults than any other infectious disease besides HIV/AIDS. Nearly 9 million new cases of TB appeared in 2003, causing perhaps 1.6 million deaths, with nine out of 10 coming in low- and middle-income countries.

Growing drug resistance suggests that the current approach might not be able to bring TB under control, especially in Africa and the former Soviet republics. Addressing resistance increases costs and the short-term benefits in saved lives are limited. This means that compared with 2008, when the costs and benefits were calculated for the last Copenhagen Consensus project, the benefits for each dollar spent are actually lower. But, with each dollar achieving more $15 worth of benefits in economic terms, TB control remains a very worthwhile investment. Spending $1.5 billion would save one million adult deaths annually.

The third approach Jamison outlines is expanding case-management of acutely ill children and adding several new antigens to routine vaccinations. These include Haemophilus influenza type b (Hib) and Streptococcus pneumonia which are common causes of childhood pneumonia; hepatitis B which protects against liver cancer; and newer rotavirus and shigella vaccines to prevent diarrhea. The Global Alliance for Vaccines and Immunization estimates that the addition of Hib and pneumococcal vaccines to vaccination programs could save 800,000 lives a year, and rotavirus and shigella vaccines might save 600,000. In total, Jamison's team estimates that spending about $1 billion annually on expanded immunization coverage would save one million child deaths annually. Put into economic terms, the benefits would be 20 times higher than the costs.

Another priority is deworming. The costs of worm treatment are low and the prevalence is high, but this remains a neglected infection. From complications with digestion to difficulty absorbing nutrients, worms can be detrimental to a person's overall well-being, hampering productivity, appetite, fitness, and growth. Children are at greater risk of infection than adults and will suffer more severe, lifelong complications if worms are left untreated. Children who experience worm infection often live in poor communities and need a sustainable treatment plan to remedy any loss in education, nutrition, and intellectual development they may experience. Spending $300 million would mean about 300 million children could be dewormed, with benefits in economic terms 10 times higher than the costs.

No disease comes close to the AIDS epidemic in threatening every aspect of development for dozens of countries. Unfortunately, it is also in many ways the hardest to tackle. Jamison's team draws on research created for the Copenhagen Consensus and Rush Foundation project RethinkHIV to identify priorities against this disease. The most effective preventive interventions against HIV are those targeting sex workers and those most likely to contribute to increased transmission, as has been done successfully in India and other Asian countries. Voluntary counseling and testing has reduced unsafe behavior in some studies, although the duration of this change is not clear. Prevention of mother-to-child infection is cheap and effective, and needle exchange and blood safety programs can reduce other modes of transmission.

An HIV vaccine is the ultimate preventative tool. The researchers use RethinkHIV research by Robert Hecht and Dean Jamison on the costs and benefits of increasing research funding to speed up the arrival of a useful vaccine. Jamison concludes that there is a strong case for increasing HIV vaccine research and development by $100 million annually. Even with conservative assumptions, each dollar spent would generate benefits worth 20 times the costs.

It is striking that most of the top five investments would largely save the lives of children. This points to a broader issue, which is inequality in health conditions. As Jamison's team notes, from 1990 to 2001, the under-5 mortality rate remained stagnant or increased in 23 countries. In another 53 countries, including China, the rate of decline in child mortality was less than half of that required to reach the Millennium Development Goal. We have had many real successes in high- and middle-income countries in the battle against infectious disease; our real challenge is spreading this success to low-income countries, and particularly to children in these areas

There are strong arguments to increase spending on infectious diseases.

CHRONIC DISEASES

The High Cost of Heart Disease and Cancer

Malaria, AIDS, and tuberculosis get all the attention in the developing world. But chronic diseases kill more people.

Chronic diseases such as heart disease, stroke, and cancer are problems that we associate with rich countries, while infectious diseases such as malaria and HIV/AIDS are more commonly seen as the problems afflicting the poor. But 80 percent of global deaths from chronic diseases occur in low-income and middle-income countries. Cardiovascular disease in low- and middle-income countries killed more than twice as many people in 2001 as did AIDS, malaria, and TB combined.

Yet, according to a recent review of donor health funding, chronic disease receives the smallest amount of donor assistance of all health conditions, having lost ground since 1990 relative to infectious diseases. Donor assistance for health was estimated at almost $26 billion in 2009. The amount allocated to chronic disease was $270 million, or a miniscule one percent of the total.

For the Copenhagen Consensus 2012, specialist academics produced new research on the smartest responses to global challenges, and then Nobel Laureate economists prioritized the best policies. In a research paper released on chronic disease, Prabhat Jha and a team of researchers argue that chronic diseases already pose a substantial economic burden, and this burden will evolve into a staggering one over the next two decades. Jha and his team argue that addressing chronic disease in poor countries requires a rethinking of developmental assistance and possibly new delivery approaches.

Although high-income countries currently bear the biggest economic burden of chronic diseases, developing countries (especially those that are middle-income) will assume an increasing share as their populations grow and the effects of the tobacco epidemic take greater hold.

And the costs for governments of achieving maximal adult survival are rising, in contrast to declines in the costs of achieving child survival. This divergence is chiefly a consequence of the lack of tobacco control in most low and middle-income countries (while smoking rates are declining in many developed countries, they are on the rise in the developing world), the lack of sustained investments in new drugs, and gaps in the strategies and in the program implementation for chronic diseases.

Jha and his team identify five key priority interventions where the costs are relatively low compared to the benefits.

The most important action is tobacco taxation. Estimating conservatively that tobacco causes about one-third of the vascular disease, half of all cancers and 60 percent of chronic respiratory diseases, the researchers estimate a total economic loss from tobacco of about $12.7 trillion over the next 20 years—or about 1.3 of global GDP annually. Already, tobacco kills up to 6 million people a year, including about one million each in China and India. Without increased cessation efforts, tobacco use could account for about 10 million deaths per year by 2030, with most of these occurring in low- and middle-income countries. With no change to current patterns, one billion tobacco deaths might occur this century, in contrast to 100 million in the 20th century.

Reducing tobacco deaths in the next few decades requires current smokers to quit, and tobacco taxation is particularly effective at raising cessation rates: a 10 percent increase in price leads to a 4 percent to 8 percent drop in consumption. France, for example, tripled the price of cigarettes quickly (over a decade or so), and this cut consumption per adult in half, while more than doubling tax revenue in real terms. Lung cancer rates for young men in France have fallen sharply since. Tax hikes need not cost anything except the political will to overcome vested interests. Generously estimating a comprehensive tobacco control program including a tobacco tax rise to cost $500 million annually, such a program would avert more than one million deaths each year. Put into economic terms, the benefits would be 40 times higher than the costs.

The second initiative is using low-cost drugs to avert heart attacks. Jha argues that systemwide efforts to achieve high rates of appropriate drug use administered within hours of an acute heart attack should be a high priority. Up to 300,000 heart-attack deaths could be prevented each year at the cost of $200 million. Jha calculates that, in economic terms, each dollar spent would generate $25 of benefits.

Another approach to the same problem is to create a "generic risk pill". In the absence of any drug therapy, adults with previous stroke, heart attack, diabetes, or any other evidence of some serious vascular disease have about a 7 percent annual risk of either dying or being rehospitalized with a recurrence. If they take an aspirin a day, that risk drops to 5 percent; if they add two more drugs to reduce blood pressure and blood lipids, it drops to 2 percent. The exact sequence of drugs matters little, but being on three or four drugs (aspirin, a blood pressure pill or two, and a statin drug to lower cholesterol) daily versus being on no drugs means a greatly reduced 10-year risk of rehospitalization: 16 percent for those receiving treatment as compared with 50 percent for those on no drugs. All of these drugs are low-cost and thus could be easily packaged into "polypills" or generic risk pills for widespread use, similar to the way many countries treat tuberculosis with several drugs.

This "generic risk pill" would prevent 1.6 million deaths annually. If the cost per adult patient per year were $100, the total cost would then be $32 billion per year. The higher cost is reflected in a lower "benefit/cost ratio": Each dollar spent on this initiative would see about $4 worth of benefits. Still, this remains an attractive investment.

Next, Jha proposes efforts to reduce salt consumption, which is a significant cause of heart diseases and strokes. This can be done in food processing or at the cooking or eating stages. The former approach is being tried in Latin America where Brazil, Argentina, and Chile are among the countries with industry agreements to reduce salt in processing.

Experience in the United Sates and other developed countries suggests that substantial reduction from current levels is feasible with only some consumer resistance. Argentina and South Africa are focusing on salt reduction in bread. The main limitation in salt reduction strategies is the unproven impact on changing behavior when salt is mostly added at the table as a condiment. The researchers propose a population-level intervention to reduce salt intake through voluntary manufacturing changes, behavior change using mass media and other awareness raising campaigns. An annual expenditure of $1 billion would save more than 1.3 million lives a year from heart disease and strokes, meaning that the benefits are 20 times higher than the costs.

Finally, Hepatitis B is a viral infection that attacks the liver and is the major cause of liver cancer worldwide. Yet the Hepatitis B vaccine can prevent 90 percent of liver cancer deaths, and the Hepatitis B vaccine is safe and very effective when given at birth or in early childhood. The vaccine could cost as little as $3.60 per child vaccinated. Spending $122 million to increase vaccine coverage by 25 percent would avert about 150,000 annual deaths from the disease, 40 years into the future. Each dollar spent generates $10 of benefits.

There is a strong argument to increase spending on chronic disease. The burden on poor countries is already high, and will grow considerably.

HUNGER AND MALNUTRITION

How To Get Food on Every Table

We have enough food to feed everyone. But we need to produce even more. Here's why.

The problem of hunger can be solved. The planet creates more than enough food to meet everyone's needs. But there are still about 925 million hungry people in the world, and nearly 180 million preschool-age children do not get vital nutrients.

In 2008, the last global Copenhagen Consensus project focused attention on the problem of hidden hunger. A team of Nobel Laureate economists found that micronutrient interventions—fortification and supplements designed to increase nutrient intake—were the most effective investment that could be made, with massive benefits for a tiny price tag.

In Copenhagen Consensus 2012, researchers and Nobel Laureates again looked at the smartest solutions to the world's biggest challenges. In a research paper on hunger and undernutrition, researchers John Hoddinott, Mark Rosegrant, and Maximo Torero of the International Food Policy Research Institute once more propose that decision-makers prioritize micronutrient interventions, and they update the analysis of the costs and benefits of doing so.

They find that for a relatively small amount of money—less than $700 million annually—it would be possible to eliminate vitamin A deficiencies in preschool-age children, eliminate iodine deficiency globally, and dramatically reduce maternal anemia during pregnancy. But they also offer new solutions, including bundling nutrition interventions, increasing global food production, and improving the economic conditions of the rural poor through better communications and increased competition in fertilizer markets.

Chronic undernutrition has significant neurological consequences that can damage spatial navigation and memory formation, leading to loss of cognitive abilities and, in time, lower incomes. Hoddinott, Rosegrant, and Torero find that for about $100 per child, a bundle of interventions (including micronutrients and improvements in diet quality and behavior) would reduce chronic undernutrition by 36 percent in developing countries. Even in very poor countries such as Ethiopia and using very conservative assumptions, each dollar spent reducing chronic undernutrition has a $30 payoff when seen in economic terms.

Increasing global food production might seem a strange proposed policy given that globally, food production actually exceeds food needs. But the researchers argue that lower prices are necessary to make food more affordable and to provide a buffer against some of the negative consequences of climate change. Hoddinott's team looks at how to speed up improvements in agricultural production. This means first and foremost increasing research and development to ensure higher yields through extensive breeding. But the researchers also look at ways to increase tolerance to drought, heat and salt, identifying and disseminating the best varieties of crops, addressing problems like wheat rust, developing resistance to cattle diseases like East Coast Fever, and focusing on soil diagnostics to ensure that optimal combinations of organic and inorganic fertilizers are used.

They propose an $8 billion to $13 billion increase in annual global public investment in agricultural research and development. (The team uses economic modeling to calculate the results on yields, incomes, GDP growth, and prices.) This investment would mean that in 2050, canola oil would be 68 percent cheaper, and rice would be nearly 25 percent cheaper than it would otherwise be. There would be 200 million fewer hungry people around the world. Taking global population growth into account, hunger would be 63 percent less prevalent in 2050 than it was in 2010, with the reduction most pronounced in South Asia and Sub-Saharan Africa. Spending an additional $8 billion per year would, by 2050, reduce the number of hungry people in the world by 210 million and the number of underweight children by 10 million. Put into economic terms, the benefit/cost ratio of this spending is 16 to 1, indicating high returns to expanded investment in agricultural R&D.

Roughly 80 percent of the global hungry live in rural areas and half are smallholders. The researchers propose a dual approach to improving the economic conditions of the rural poor, by providing market information through cellphones and reducing barriers to fertilizer access.

In India, the Reuters Market Light program sends text messages to smallholders with crop advice. The monthly cost is $1.50, and recipients get configurable, location-specific weather forecasts, local price information, and local and international commodity information. Hoddinott looks at African and south-Asian studies into the impact of improved market information, and concludes that with the most pessimistic assumptions this investment can be justified only in a few countries. But under any other set of assumptions, benefits will exceed costs and in some cases do so by a considerable factor, up to 8.35 in return for every dollar spent.

There have been mixed results from policies designed to stimulate sustainable fertilizer use, but Hoddinott's team notes that not much has been said about developing regions and their increasing dependence on imported fertilizer. A small number of countries control most of the production capacity for the main nitrogen, phosphate, and potash fertilizers. In most cases, the top four firms control more than half of each country's production capacity. Policymakers could consider forcing the breakup of this concentrated industry. But apart from the disruption this would cause, this could lead to a loss of economies of scale. Regulation is another possibility, but imposing price restrictions could lead to unproductive rent-seeking. Instead, the researchers propose investment in the construction of new production capacity. Private companies are deterred from entering the market by high fixed costs and strategic pricing behavior by incumbents, so the researchers outline a case for public investment in production capacity with the understanding that the operation of the facility would be turned over to the private sector. Hoddinott estimates that building fertilizer plants with annual production capacity high enough to be a top-four firm would cost $1.2 billion in South Asia and $700 million in Africa. Put into economic terms, the net present value of doing so is $12.5 billion.

CORRUPTION AND TRADE BARRIERS

There are two more research papers, which are devoted to major global challenges whose solutions are largely political rather than a matter of spending more money. The challenge papers on Corruption and Trade Barriers were considered by the Expert Panel, who comment on them. They include cost and benefit estimates, but lack concrete investment proposals. Their inclusion here is to highlight the benefits of responding to these challenges, as well as outline the barriers and implementation issues.

Corruption

Susan Rose-Ackerman and Rory Truex examine different solutions to tackle corruption.

The authors caution that, at present, there is a lack of good data on the relative effectiveness of most reform programs. Yet, even without definitive studies, some options look promising because benefits seem clear and the costs are minimal. Even if the benefits cannot be precisely measured, the rates of return appear large.

Perhaps the most often prescribed remedy for corruption is to increase top-down monitoring and punishment. Improved monitoring, whether in the form of an external auditor, an anti-corruption agency, or an international oversight body, increases the probability of being caught. There is some evidence that increased monitoring does have positive effects on government performance.

The natural complements to external monitoring and punishment by formal organization are increased transparency and bottom-up accountability. Citizens have an interest in fighting corruption, and if given a voice, they can be a potent force for its reduction. In 2004, the Ugandan government began publishing the details of education funding processes in local newspapers, allowing citizens and schoolmasters to better monitor the release of funds from higher levels of government. The analysis shows that communities with better access to newspapers, as well as more informed schoolmasters, experienced lower leakage rates, and that the introduction of the newspaper campaign as a whole substantially reduced leakage rates and associated embezzlement. The release of such vital information to citizens may require little more than a website or a well-placed newspaper story, and the potential returns may be quite large.

Internal bureaucratic reorganization and the improved administration of public programs are equally, if not more, important to the anti-corruption calculus. If bureaucrats have easy access to rents, an abundance of corrupt partners, and a low public service ethos, self-dealing is nearly inevitable. Internal reforms, such as meritocratic recruitment and competitive public salaries, can help ensure that those situations do not occur.

When the state carries out large-scale projects, signs contracts, and sells assets, such deals produce substantial financial gains that are difficult to monitor. Hence, grand corruption may be a serious problem. Reforms in this category could include both more competitive and transparent bidding processes and careful evaluation of what is being bought and sold in order to be sure that these choices are not distorted by self-dealing officials.

However, if government bodies are riddled with corruption and inefficiency, a final drastic remedy is to remove certain tasks from the public sector completely, moving their provision to the private sector. Firms have taken over basic service provision in parts of India, tax collection in Uganda, transportation in Mexico City and parts of customs inspection in over fifty developing countries. The existing record suggests that privatization is a high risk, high reward strategy— some reforms seem to have substantially reduced corruption; others appear to have made the situation worse.

The authors stress the need to focus not only on controls inside states where corrupt deals occur but also on international forums. At the international level, reforms should go beyond the weak enforcement mechanisms in existing treaties and contracts.

Trade barriers

Kym Anderson looks at the barriers to international trade in goods, services, and in capital flows. Such policies hurt the economies imposing them, but are particularly harmful to the world's poorest people.

Anderson argues that addressing this challenge would therefore also reduce poverty and thereby assist in meeting several of the other challenges identified in this project, including malnutrition, disease, poor education and air pollution.

The challenge involves finding politically attractive ways to phase out remaining distortions to world markets for goods and services. Kym Anderson focuses on how costly those anti-poor trade policies are, and examines possible strategies to reduce remaining distortions. He addresses four opportunities in particular.

Among the most feasible opportunities available today for encouraging trade negotiations to stimulate significant market opening, the most obvious is a non-preferential legally binding partial liberalization of goods and services trade following the WTO's current round of multilateral trade negotiations, the Doha Development Agenda.

The net present value of the future benefits of a Doha agreement ranges from $12 trillion to $64 trillion. The costs are less than $400 billion in present value terms, but they are mostly private rather than government costs and are dwarfed by the gross benefits. Today's developing countries would reap just over half of those net gains, as their share of the global economy is assumed to grow throughout this century (although at a progressively slower rate after 2025). Their benefit/cost ratios from the trade reform opportunity offered by the Doha round are between 140 and 250, which means it is an extremely high payoff activity, if only the political will to bring about a successful conclusion to the Doha round can be found. The global benefit/cost ratios from Doha are not much lower, at between 90 and 180.

If for political reasons the Doha round cannot be brought to a successful conclusion with all the flexibilities demanded by developing countries, governments still have the opportunity to form preferential trade agreements.

One involves the proposed Trans-Pacific Partnership (TPP) among a subset of member countries of the Asia Pacific Economic Cooperation (APEC) grouping. Another sub-regional agreement involves extending the free-trade area among the 10-member Association of South East Asian Nations to include China, Japan and Korea (ASEAN+3).

The third opportunity is a free-trade area among all APEC countries. APEC leaders have endorsed both the Trans-Pacific Partnership and ASEAN+3 integration tracks and see them as potential pathways to a free trade agreement involving all APEC members.

Of the three possibilities among countries in the Asia-Pacific region, the greatest estimated gain would come if all APEC member countries agreed to form a region-wide free-trade area (FTAAP).

That is assumed to involve completely freeing all trade, albeit preferentially within the Asia-Pacific region (including Russia). This stands in contrast to a Doha agreement, which would only partially open up trade, albeit non-preferentially so that all trading partners are involved (as the WTO membership now includes nearly 160 members and thus almost all of world trade).

Since the APEC members are projected to comprise nearly three-fifths of global GDP by 2025, it is not surprising that a free trade agreement among them could yield a benefit to the world that is three-quarters of what Doha is projected to deliver. Furthermore, the FTAAP is projected to deliver a slightly greater benefit to developing countries as a group than is Doha. This is partly because under Doha, developing countries are assumed to reform less than high-income countries, and partly because by 2025 the APEC grouping will account for around two-thirds of the GDP of all developing countries.

The two other opportunities analyzed by Anderson involve sub-regional free trade agreements in the Asia-Pacific region, and so necessarily yield smaller benefits than a free trade agreement for the entire APEC region: fewer countries are liberalizing, and only for their trade with a subset of APEC members. Of those two, the ASEAN+3 proposal would yield more than twice the global and developing country benefits as the Trans-Pacific Partnership between the US and a number of small APEC economies.

RANKING
THE OPPORTUNITIES

BIG PROBLEMS, BIG SOLUTIONS—
YOU NEED TO TAKE A STAND

By Bjørn Lomborg

This decade has seen remarkable progress against humanity's greatest challenges. Consider the declaration of victory over polio in India, which seemed impossible 10 years ago. January 2014 marked three years since the country's last reported case. Or look at the strides made against malaria: Over the past decade, the number of cases has been reduced by 17 percent, and the number of deaths has dropped by 26 percent.

Despite global population growth and economic crisis, absolute poverty—the proportion of people living on less than $1.25 a day—is falling in every region of the world. In fact, the United Nations Millennium Development Goal of cutting extreme poverty in half has been achieved five years ahead of time.

Just a few years ago, the use of male circumcision as a tool in the fight against HIV/AIDS was largely unknown. Today, UNAIDS and the World Health Organization recommend it as a means to combat HIV/AIDS, and more than 10 African countries are implementing strategies to increase its availability. Similarly, the concept of using geoengineering to respond to climate change has moved from science fiction to an area of serious research.

This decade has also witnessed a 60 percent increase in global development aid. Bill Gates' Giving Pledge challenge has graduated from concept to campaign, with at least $125 billion promised to good causes.

But, while the last decade has given much reason for cheer, there are areas in which we cannot claim such success. Climate change has emerged as one of the most discussed problems, yet global negotiations have fallen apart, and we are barely any closer to cutting carbon emissions than we were 10 years ago.

Similarly, violent conflicts continue to take a toll that is far too high. And, while the world met the Millennium Development Goal for providing clean drinking water five years early, the provision of sanitation has fallen behind: An astonishing one-third of the world's population, 2.5 billion people, lack access to basic sanitation, and more than one billion people still defecate in the open.

Other problems have emerged and grown over the decade. If current patterns continue, tobacco use may account for some 10 million deaths per year by 2030, with most occurring in low- and middle-income countries: We might see roughly one billion tobacco-related deaths in this century, compared to 100 million in the 20th century. Cardiovascular diseases account for 13 million deaths in low- and middle-income countries each year, more than a quarter of the entire death toll, and risk factors are growing.

The state of challenges facing humanity changes rapidly. So does our knowledge of how best to respond. Policymakers and philanthropists need access to regularly updated information on how to use limited funds effectively.

The Copenhagen Consensus project, which I direct, provides a link between academic research and concrete economic analysis that can be used by decision-makers in the real world. Every four years, researchers and Nobel Laureates work to identify the smartest responses to the biggest problems facing humanity.

In 2004, the Copenhagen Consensus highlighted the need to prioritize measures to control and treat HIV/AIDS. More money and attention was soon devoted to HIV prevention and treatment. In 2008, the Copenhagen Consensus focused the attention of policymakers and philanthropists on investments in micronutrient provision. Public acceptance of this idea led to an increase in efforts to reduce "hidden hunger"— that is, people suffering from not getting the nutrients that they need.

In May 2012, more than 30 Nobel Laureates and researchers worked together once again to identify the smartest ways to respond to global challenges, based on the latest information about the toughest problems facing our world.

Since 2008, the global economic crisis has made it even more necessary to ensure that development and aid spending is used wisely, where it can make the biggest difference. The Copenhagen Consensus project carried out the difficult task of comparing one set of initiatives with another by using fundamental economic tools and principles.

First, teams of world-renowned expert economists wrote research papers on the costs and benefits of a range of investments that address specific challenges. Debate and discussion was encouraged by ensuring that three papers are written for each topic, so a range of expert opinions is made available. This provides the framework for this book, in which we can see the full price tag, incorporating all of the costs, benefits, and spin-offs to society from using a limited amount of money in a particular way.

All of this research constitutes a valuable contribution to international development and aid policy. But the project went a step further. A panel of the world's top economists—including four Nobel Laureates—vetted and debated the experts' recommendations, and identified the most attractive possibilities. Alongside the research papers, the Nobel Laureates' prioritized list provides an important input for policymakers and philanthropists.

While the past decade has witnessed much progress and reason for hope, there are still many important problems to tackle: malnutrition, sanitation, education, civil conflicts, climate change, and natural disasters, to name some of the most prominent.

But are the most prominent problems necessarily those that we should address immediately? The research and the prioritized list make us consider the reasons for our current priorities, and challenge us to spend limited resources to do the most good first. And what are the best things to do first?

While we had expert economists develop a prioritized list, at the same time Slate readers had an opportunity to answer this question themselves. Over two weeks, I presented the summaries published in this book.

In each of the 10 articles, I outlined the latest thinking on the smartest ways to respond to one global challenge, on the same day that each research paper was released to the public. I asked Slate readers, each day, for their views about that day's choices. Would you rather policy-makers prioritized efforts to improve agricultural output, for example, or that they invested more in micronutrient interventions in developing countries?

In this process I discovered what investments Slate readers would prioritize to continue to make rapid progress against the planet's biggest challenges.

Slate Readers' ranking

For nearly every single investment presented in this book and to Slate's readers, the benefits were greater than the costs, meaning that these were almost all investments that would undeniably help the planet. But, with limited funds, we need to start somewhere, and the Copenhagen Consensus 2012 project challenged you to think about where you would—and wouldn't—direct additional funds first.

While Slate readers were considering the research, a team of economists (including four Nobel Laureates) did the same in Copenhagen. They, of course, had examined draft versions of the papers and also considered the findings from two additional research papers for every topic. (These were the so-called "perspective papers," which we use to provide a transparent critique of the original research. All of these papers can be found in the book *Global Problems, Smart Solutions* (Cambridge University Press, 2013).

The Copenhagen Consensus 2012 "expert panel" had the advantage of being able to interview the authors and to bounce ideas off of one another before coming up with a consensus priority list. (The comments section on Slate allowed me to have conversations with the readers about the research papers; I've endeavored to answer many of the questions in sidebar articles throughout the series.) The expert panel also had the opportunity to choose not to prioritize some interventions, or to bundle different priorities together. You can read the panel's explainations to all of the thinking behind each of the priority choices they made in this book; I think it's a must-read that shows us how we could effectively achieve much more in the fight against humanity's biggest challenges.

Let's turn to the rankings by Slate readers. Here they are:

Rank	Solution	Challenge
1	Family Planning	Population Growth
2	Bundled Micro-Nutrient Interventions	Hunger and Malnutrition
3	Tobacco Taxation	Chronic Diseases
4	Civil War Prevention	Armed Conflicts
5	Schoolbased Health and Nutrition Programs	Education
6	Effective Early Warning Systems	Natural Disasters
7	Expanded Childhood Immunization Coverage	Infectious Disease
8	The Reinvented Toilet	Water and Sanitation
9	Increased Funding for Energy R&D	Climate Change
10	Agricultural Productivity R&D	Biodiversity
11	Subsidy for Malaria Combination Treatment	Infectious Disease
12	R&D to Increase Yield Enhancements	Hunger and Malnutrition
13	Hepatitis B Immunization	Chronic Diseases
14	Deworming of Children	Infectious Disease
15	Geo-Engineering R&D	Climate Change
16	Extension of Protected areas	Biodiversity
17	Community Led Total Sanitation	Water and Sanitation
18	Protecting All Forests	Biodiversity
19	Expanding Tuberculosis Treatment	Infectious Disease
20	Adaptation Planning	Climate Change
21	Acute Heart Attack Low-Cost Drugs	Chronic Diseases
22	Post-Conflict Reconstruction	Armed Conflicts
23	Low$1.8/tC Global Carbon Tax	Climate Change
24	Retrofitting Schools to Withstand Earthquake Damage	Natural Disasters
25	Generic Pill for Heart Attack Risk Reduction	Chronic Diseases
26	Investing in Accelerated HIV Vaccine Development	Infectious Disease
27	Information Campaign on Returns to Schooling	Education
28	Sanitation as a Business	Water and Sanitation
29	Strengthening Structures Against Hurricanes and Storms	Natural Disasters
30	Community Walls Against Floods	Natural Disasters
31	Conditional Cash Transfers for School Attendance	Education
32	Increase Competition in the Fertilizer Market	Hunger and Malnutrition
33	Salt Reduction Campaign	Chronic Diseases
34	Crop Advisory Text Messages	Hunger and Malnutrition
35	Civil War Intervention	Armed Conflicts
36	High $250/tC Global Carbon Tax	Climate Change

This is a striking set of priorities. As we can see in the following section, Slate readers agree with the Nobel Laureates (and with the cost/benefit analysis itself) that the bundled micronutrient interventions are of great importance, both in the battle against hunger and in the endeavor to keep more kids in school.

There is agreement, also, on the importance of setting up early warning systems in developing nations to better protect populations from natural disasters. Both groups agree that it is important to expand childhood immunization coverage and to keep making malaria medicines affordable.

But there are some fascinating differences, as well. The concept of "overpopulation" was a very polarizing one in the Slate reader comments, and it was raised in connection with almost every single challenge. We looked at research that focuses on filling the "unmet need": reaching those women who want to stop having children (or delay their next childbirth) but are not on contraception. This immediately shot to the top of our poll and, despite vigorous voting on other proposals, never slipped from the "top priority" slot.

The Nobel Laureates ranked this lower, based on concerns about the feasibility of actually filling all of the "unmet need"; they felt that a better approach would be to first zero-in on the households that were easier to reach.

Tobacco taxation was very popular with Slate readers. The Copenhagen Consensus panel gave this a lower ranking, based on the belief that, while this was undeniably an effective intervention, it was largely a question of political will rather than funds.

And the concept of the "reinvented toilet" was liked by Slate readers, but the expert panel noted that this was a long time away from availability, involving research and development lasting 15 to 20 years followed by marketing, with an unclear pathway to success. While it's a noble goal, attempts to calculate costs and benefits are highly speculative, and the necessary seed money has already been allocated by the Gates Foundation.

In conclusion, costs and benefits shouldn't drive our decisions, but they are an important consideration to take into account. The goal of the Copenhagen Consensus is to challenge preconceptions about aid and development spending choices. We provide a base of economic evidence on which we can improve our decisions. There is no decision more important than how to best step up the fight against humanity's biggest challenges.

EXPERT PANEL RANKING

By Finn E. Kydland, Robert Mundell,
Thomas Schelling, Vernon Smith, Nancy Stokey

The goal of Copenhagen Consensus 2012 was to set priorities among a series of proposals for confronting ten of the world's most important challenges. These challenges were examined: Armed Conflict, Biodiversity, Chronic Disease, Climate Change, Education, Hunger and Malnutrition, Infectious Disease, Natural Disasters, Population Growth and Water and Sanitation, detailed in the previous section.

A panel of economic experts, comprising five of the world's most distinguished economists, was invited to consider these issues. The members were:

- Finn E. Kydland, University of California, Santa Barbara (Nobel Laureate)
- Robert Mundell, Columbia University in New York (Nobel Laureate)
- Thomas Schelling, University of Maryland (Nobel Laureate)
- Vernon Smith, Chapman University (Nobel Laureate)
- Nancy Stokey, University of Chicago

The panel was asked to address the ten challenge areas and to answer the question: "What are the best ways of advancing global welfare, and particularly the welfare of developing countries, illustrated by supposing that an additional $75 billion of resources were at their disposal over a 4-year initial period?"

Methodology

Ten Challenge Papers, commissioned from acknowledged authorities in each area of policy, set out 39 proposals for the panel's consideration. The panel examined these proposals in detail. Each paper was discussed at length with its principal author. The panel was also informed by 14 Perspective Papers, providing critical appraisals of each Challenge Paper's assumptions and methodology. Based on the costs and benefits of the solutions, the panel ranked the proposals, in descending order of desirability.

In ordering the proposals, the panel was guided predominantly by consideration of economic costs and benefits. After in-depth review of the papers, and question-and-answer sessions between the panel experts and the researchers, each panelist came up with their own personal rankings. These rankings were then aggregated based on a median vote. The panel acknowledged the difficulties that cost/benefit analysis must overcome, both in principle and as a practical matter, but agreed that the cost/benefit approach was an indispensable organizing method. In setting priorities, the panel took account of the strengths and weaknesses of the specific cost/benefit appraisals under review, and gave weight both to the institutional preconditions for success and to the demands of ethical or humanitarian urgency. As a general matter, the panel noted that higher standards of governance and improvements in the institutions required to support development in the world's poor countries are of paramount importance.

For some of the proposals, the panel found that information was too sparse to allow a judgment to be made. These proposals, some of which might prove valuable after further study, were therefore excluded from the ranking. Details of this can be found in the following section 'Notes about the Challenges'.

Each expert assigned his or her own ranking to the proposals. The individual rankings, together with commentaries prepared by each expert can be found in the following sections of this book. The panel's ranking was calculated by taking the median of individual rankings. The panel jointly endorses the median ordering shown above as representing their agreed view.

Final Prioritized Ranking

	Challenge	Solution
1	Hunger & Education	Bundled Interventions to Reduce Undernutrition in Pre-Schoolers
2	Infectious Disease	Subsidy for Malaria Combination Treatment
3	Infectious Disease	Expanded Childhood Immunization Coverage
4	Infectious Disease	Deworming of Schoolchildren
5	Infectious Disease	Expanding Tuberculosis Treatment
6	Hunger & Biodiversity & Climate Change	R&D to Increase Yield Enhancements
7	Natural Disasters	Investing in Effective Early Warning Systems
8	Infectious Disease	Strengthening Surgical Capacity
9	Chronic Disease	Hepatitis B Immunization
10	Chronic Disease	Acute Heart Attack Low-Cost Drugs
11	Chronic Disease	Salt Reduction Campaign
12	Climate Change	Geo-Engineering R&D
13	Education	Conditional Cash Transfers for School Attendance
14	Infectious Disease	Accelerated HIV Vaccine R&D
15	Education	Information Campaign on Benefits From Schooling
16	Water and Sanitation	Borehole and Public Hand Pump Intervention
17	Climate Change	Increased Funding for Green Energy R&D
18	Population Growth	Increase Availability of Family Planning
19	Chronic Disease	Heart Attack Risk Reduction Generic Pill
20	Water and Sanitation	Community Led Total Sanitation
21	Water and Sanitation	Sanitation as a Business
22	Chronic Disease	Increasing Tobacco Taxation
23	Natural Disasters	Community Walls Against Floods
24	Water and Sanitation	The Reinvented Toilet
25	Biodiversity	Protecting All Forests
26	Natural Disasters	Retrofitting Schools to Withstand Earthquake Damage
27	Hunger	Crop Advisory Text Messages
28	Biodiversity	Extension of Protected Areas
29	Natural Disasters	Strengthening Structures Against Hurricanes and Storms
30	Natural Disasters	Elevating Residential Structures to Avoid Flooding

Budget

The expert panel based its budget allocations on the proposals from authors, and on their own views of appropriate expenditure.

Solution	Amount Allocated Per Year, in $US Billion
Bundled Interventions to Reduce Undernutrition in Pre-Schoolers	3.0
Subsidy for Malaria Combination Treatment	0.3
Expanded Childhood Immunization Coverage	1.0
Deworming of Schoolchildren	0.3
Expanding Tuberculosis Treatment	1.5
R&D to Increase Yield Enhancements	2.0
Investing in Effective Early Warning Systems	1.0
Strengthening Surgical Capacity	3.0
Hepatitis B Immunization	0.12
Acute Heart Attack Low-Cost Drugs	0.2
Salt Reduction Campaign	1.0
Geo-Engineering R&D	1.0
Conditional Cash Transfers for School Attendance*	1.0
Accelerated HIV Vaccine R&D	0.1
Information Campaign on Benefits From Schooling*	1.34
Borehole and Public Hand Pump Intervention	1.89
Total	**$18.75**

*Estimate

Notes about the Challenges

Hunger and Malnutrition

The expert panel examined the following solutions to this challenge: Interventions to Reduce Chronic Undernutrition in Pre-Schoolers, R&D to Increase Yield Enhancements, Crop Advisory Text Messages, Increase Competition in the Fertilizer Market.

Based on very high benefit/cost ratios, the Expert Panel chose to give its highest ranking to Interventions to Reduce Chronic Undernutrition in Pre-Schoolers. The expert panel merged this with a similar proposed investment contained in the Education paper. For about $100 per child, this bundle of interventions (including micronutrient provision, and also complementary foods, treatments for worms and diarrheal diseases, and behavior change programs), could reduce chronic undernutrition by 36 percent in developing countries. The expert panel noted that the educational benefits as well as the health benefits should be taken into consideration. Even in very poor countries and using very conservative assumptions, each dollar spent reducing chronic undernutrition has at least a $30 payoff.

The Expert Panel merged the intervention of R&D to Increase Yield Enhancements with the similar investment from the Biodiversity topic. The Expert Panel noted accordingly that this investment would not lead only to a reduction in hunger, but also created benefits stemming from its effects on Biodiversity and Climate Change. The benefit/cost ratios are therefore very respectable for this intervention.

The expert panel gave a comparatively low ranking to Crop Advisory Text Messages, reflecting that this service is probably best left handled locally and by the private market.

In line with the unavailability of benefit/cost ratios for the solution of Increasing Competition in the Fertilizer Market, and the author's views that this was not as promising as it had first appeared, the expert panel chose not to rank it, while still emphasizing it as a relevant research consideration.

Education

The expert panel examined the following solutions to this challenge: School-Based Health and Nutrition Programs, Conditional Cash Transfers for School Attendance, Information Campaign on Benefits From Schooling (Extended Field Trial).

The first investment considered, School-Based Health and Nutrition Programs, shared many features with the Interventions to Reduce Chronic Undernutrition in Pre-Schoolers under the heading of Hunger and Malnutrition. As a result, the expert panel combined these interventions into one investment proposal; further discussion of that investment is included above, under the heading of Hunger and Malnutrition.

The expert panel gave mid-rankings to the other two proposals considered. They found that there were considerable benefits to using conditional cash transfers to increase school attendance in some settings, and that there was a strong case to prioritize funding for an extended field trial of an information campaign on the benefits from schooling.

Infectious Disease

The expert panel examined the following solutions to this challenge: Subsidy for Malaria Combination Treatment, Expanded Childhood Immunization Coverage, Deworming of Schoolchildren, Expanding Tuberculosis Treatment, Strengthening Surgical Capacity, Accelerated HIV Vaccine R&D.

The expert panel was impressed by the high benefit/cost ratios for the Infectious Disease solutions, even with conservative assumptions used.

A high priority for additional spending is to reduce the relative prices that poor countries face for new artemisinin combination therapies (through the so-called "Affordable Medicines Facility-malaria"). Every $1 million spent on this financing mechanism of the Global Fund means about 300,000 more children treated, 20,000 of whom with severe malaria. This would prevent 1,000 deaths. Thus, spending $300 million a year on the Subsidy for Malaria Combination Treatment would prevent 300,000 child deaths, with benefits, put in economic terms, that are 35 times higher than the costs. This analysis suggests it is one of the best returns on health that could be made globally.

Another high priority is Expanded Childhood Immunization Treatment, where spending about $1 billion annually would save one million child deaths and have benefits 20 times higher than the costs.

The expert panel noted that the benefits from Deworming of Schoolchildren would not just come from the health effects, but also from making education more productive.

While the benefits for Expanding Tuberculosis Treatment are lower than in the Copenhagen Consensus 2008, this remains a very worthwhile investment.

The expert panel noted a compelling need to Strengthen Surgical Capacity in the developing world, where very low-cost investments could be highly effective.

The expert panel noted while there might be a considerable delay before an HIV vaccine is ready, this was a relatively cheap investment worthy of funds.

Biodiversity

The expert panel examined the following solutions to this challenge: Agricultural Productivity R&D, Extension of Protected Areas, Protecting All Dense Forests.

The expert panel chose to merge Agricultural Productivity R&D with the similar intervention proposed under the topic of Hunger and Malnutrition, noting the combined benefits of this investment; discussion of this intervention is included under that heading above.

The expert panel questions the political viability of Protecting All Dense Forests over a 30-year period. It is not clear that many countries are able to prevent forests from being converted to agriculture today; it is unclear that the investment would achieve this.

The expert panel found that Extension of Protected Areas would have obvious benefits but also significant costs, principally the loss of output from the land that is taken out of use. The low benefit/cost ratio is reflected by its low ranking by the panel. The panel also notes that many of the benefits would be more relevant to the developed world, rather than developing nations.

Natural Disasters

The expert panel examined the following solutions to this challenge: Investing in Effective Early Warning Systems, Community Walls Against Floods, Retrofitting Schools to Withstand Earthquake Damage, Strengthening Structures Against Hurricanes and Storms, Elevating Residential Structures to Avoid Flooding.

Investing in Effective Early Warning Systems was given a high ranking; it was substantially less costly, and more implementable than other interventions proposed for this topic, while it reaped significant benefits, not only from infrastructure damage reduction, but also from potentially large, reduced economic knock-on effects.

Of the two proposals to elevate structures and community walls (Community Walls Against Floods, and Elevating Residential Structures to Avoid Flooding), the expert panel noted that the Community Wall was substantially more effective. However, both were very uncertain investments and hence were ranked low. The expert panel also pointed out that a case-by-case approach was probably more useful than an overarching, global strategy. The expert panel further noted the substantial challenges inherent building sea walls, including the long timeframes required for planning, agreement, and construction.

Based on the research presented, the expert panel found that a global plan to Retrofit Schools to Withstand Earthquake Damage had a quite low cost/benefit ratio and while well-intentioned was therefore given a low ranking.

Strengthening Structures Against Hurricanes and Storms was given a low ranking by the expert panel in keeping with the relatively modest benefit/cost ratios calculated by the authors.

Chronic Disease

The expert panel examined the following solutions to this challenge: Hepatitis B Immunization, Acute Heart Attack Low-Cost Drugs, Salt Reduction Campaign, Heart Attack Risk Reduction Generic Pill, Increasing Tobacco Taxation.

Hepatitis B immunization appears to be a straight-forward and solid proposal, which the panel finds worthy of investment.

Acute Heart Attack Low-Cost Drugs was a worthy investment, but seemed to be most relevant in countries in which infrastructure was already in place, suggesting there could be some challenges in low-income countries with less health care infrastructure.

Higher awareness of the risk factors of salt consumption is important, and the expert panel found that there was a need for developed world experience in Salt Reduction Campaigns to be shared with lower income nations. This is a relatively low-cost intervention. Compared to Tobacco Taxation, salt reduction campaigns should face fewer barriers.

The Heart Attack Risk Reduction Generic Pill was a rather expensive proposal at $32 billion per year, with a respectable but not high benefit/cost ratio.

The expert panel found that Tobacco Taxation was largely a question of political will rather than funds. They noted that a gradual tax was not ideal, and that this was a highly effective response to the health problems caused by smoking. They noted that the proposed solution was more than simply taxation, but also included an information campaign which they found was important. Developed world experience with tobacco control must be shared with developing nations.

Climate Change

The expert panel examined the following solutions to this challenge: Geo-engineering R&D, Increased Funding for Green Energy R&D, Low Global Carbon Tax, High Global Carbon Tax, Adaptation Planning.

The expert panel found that geo-engineering research and development, at low cost, was worthy of some funds, to explore the costs, benefits, and risks of this technology.

The panel found the Green Energy R&D should be started at a lower level than that proposed, of $1 billion annually, which would likely imply a higher BCR. According to the Challenge Paper authors, the money should be distributed to the top green technology countries, e.g. US, Canada, UK, Germany, France, Brazil, China, India, Japan, Korea, Russia, through cross-national research consortia, focusing on financing R&D across a portfolio of technologies.

While the expert panel chose not to rank the carbon tax, it finds that a low carbon tax (around $5/ton CO_2, $19/ton C, which is the damage estimate) increasing over time, would be a sensible policy that could help address the climate change challenge. The expert panel also recognizes that without significant technological breakthrough, significant CO_2 reduction remains unlikely.

The expert panel also chose not to rank the adaptation investment solution, but underscored the importance of adaptation in the future to decrease the vulnerability of the developing world to climate change.

Water and Sanitation

The expert panel examined the following solutions to this challenge: Borehole and Public Hand Pump Intervention, Community Led Total Sanitation, Sanitation as a Business, The Reinvented Toilet.

The solid but relatively modest benefit/cost ratios of Borehole and Public Hand Pump Intervention led to its mid-ranking.

The expert panel noted that Community Led Total Sanitation was a 'road-tested' solution meaning that it carries a high degree of certainty in its ability to be expanded, as there is a good deal of previous experience and knowledge of its risks, costs, and benefits in different environments. However, like the Borehole and Public Hand Pump Intervention, it had relatively low benefit/cost ratios.

They noted that Sanitation as a Business appeared to have a relatively short timeframe to becoming available. In contrast, The Reinvented Toilet was a considerably longer time away from availability, involving research and development lasting 15-20 years followed by marketing, with an unclear pathway to success. The panel concluded that The Reinvented Toilet was a noble goal, but analysis of its costs and benefits remained highly speculative, while the necessary seed money had already been allocated by the Gates Foundation.

Population Growth

The expert panel examined the following solution to this challenge: Increase Availability of Family Planning.

The expert panel recognizes the importance of meeting the unmet need for family planning. They note that some households would be easier to reach with family planning services, and recommend that attention is focused on these households first.

Armed Conflict

The expert panel examined the following solutions to this challenge: Conflict Prevention, Conflict Intervention, Post-Conflict Reconstruction.

The expert panel chose not to include these interventions in its prioritized list. Conflict prevention is clearly important: peace is not an end to be achieved at the end of a conflict, but should be preserved. However, as with the solutions to Trade Barriers and Corruption, this topic is largely political, rather than an economic question of resource allocation. The expert panel notes that the research paper makes a valuable contribution to identifying the costs and benefits of responding to conflicts.

Corruption and Trade Barriers

Two Working Papers were commissioned by Copenhagen Consensus 2012 on corruption and reducing trade barriers. The Expert panel notes the importance of responding to both of these challenges, but notes that the barriers to response are political rather than financial in nature.

Corruption can have crippling effects on development and human welfare. There is a lack of good data on the relative effectiveness of most reform programs. Yet, even without definitive studies, some options look promising because benefits seem clear and the costs are minimal. Even if the benefits cannot be precisely measured, the rates of return appear large. Collectively, improving top-down monitoring and punishment, fostering transparency and citizen involvement, adjusting bureaucratic incentives through civil service reforms, improving the competitiveness of government asset sales and large purchases, and privatizing certain government services may provide the shock needed to push a country or sector towards a self-fulfilling cycle of good governance.

Because under freer trade the world's resources would be allocated more efficiently, the expert panel finds that cuts in trade barriers and subsidies would provide a means for citizens to spend more on other pressing problems, thereby indirectly contributing to opportunities to alleviate other challenges facing the world. The net present value of the future benefits of a Doha agreement ranges from $12 trillion to $64 trillion. The costs are less than $400 billion in present value terms, but they are mostly private rather than government costs and are dwarfed by the gross benefits.

Individual ranking by Finn E. Kydland

	Solution
1	Geo-Engineering R&D
2	Bundled Micro-Nutrient Interventions
3	Sanitation as a Business
4	R&D to Increase Yield Enhancements
5	Increase Availability of Family Planning
6	Strengthening Surgical Capacity
7	Subsidy for Malaria Combination Treatment
8	Deworming of Schoolchildren
9	Expanded Childhood Immunization Coverage
10	Investing in Effective Early Warning Systems
11	Acute Heart Attack Low-Cost Drugs
12	Conditional Cash Transfers for School Attendance
13	Expanding Tuberculosis Treatment
14	The Reinvented Toilet
15	Information Campaign on Benefits From Schooling
16	Borehole and Public Hand Pump Intervention
17	Increased Funding for Green Energy R&D
18	Salt Reduction Campaign
19	Community Led Total Sanitation
20	Accelerated HIV Vaccine R&D
21	Heart Attack Risk Reduction Generic Pill
22	Hepatitis B Immunization
23	Community Walls Against Floods
24	Retrofitting Schools to Withstand Earthquake Damage
25	Protecting All Forests
26	Crop Advisory Text Messages
27	Increasing Tobacco Taxation
28	Elevating Residential Structures to Avoid Flooding
29	Strengthening Structures Against Hurricanes and Storms
30	Extension of Protected Areas

Ten of the first 11 solutions on the panel's ranking are related to hunger and diseases. Implementing these solutions would be hugely important not only in saving lives and preventing various forms of agony among millions of people, but also in making educational attainment much more efficient and beneficial in the longer run. Personally I felt that this time, in comparison with four years ago, the estimates of benefit/cost (BC) ratios had become more accurate and credible, removing some of the uncertainty that otherwise might make one reluctant to rank a particular solution highly.

Rather than talk in detail about these solutions (I'm sure others will), let me focus on the two for which the discrepancy between my ranking and that of the overall panel was the greatest. One is "Increase Availability of Family Planning," ranked #5 by me and #18 by the panel. While population growth doesn't seem to be a global problem any more (Malthusian outlook outdated), the micro problem is that so many women don't have access to any kind of birth control. This is a huge problem for female education, productivity, and income, and is a financial burden when kids aren't affordable. My reading from the experts is that estimates from smaller programs suggest the reduction in child and maternal mortality yields B/C ratios of 30:1 to 50:1. Estimates for larger programs that could change population dynamics predict significant impacts on GDP per capita. Reductions of population growth rates of 1% could increase the growth rate of GDP per capita by about 1% in high-fertility countries. This suggests B/C ratios of 50:1 to 100:1. Combining the above analyses yields overall B/C ratios ranging from a little under to well over 100:1.

Admittedly, there is a great deal of uncertainty associated with such estimates. It's natural that different panel members take that into account to various degrees. In my case, it was hard not to be influenced by something the others hadn't seen, namely a research paper by two of my most respected colleagues at UC Santa Barbara, Henning Bohn and Charles Stuart, entitled "Global Warming and the Population Externality." According to their abstract:

"We calculate the harm a birth imposes on others when greenhouse gas emissions are a problem and a cap limits emissions damage. This negative population externality, which equals the corrective Pigovian tax on having a child, is substantial in calibrations. In our base case, the Pigovian tax is 21 percent of a parent's lifetime income in steady state and 5 percent of lifetime income immediately after imposition of a cap, per child. The optimal population in steady state, which maximizes utility taking account of the externality, is about one quarter of the population households would choose voluntarily."

As always, such estimates are only as reliable as the model and the data on which they're based. But even much lower estimates would be worthy of note.

The largest ranking discrepancy, however, was for the solution "Sanitation as a Business," ranked #3 by me and #21 overall by the panel. (The reader may recall that, as the basis for the panel ranking was medians of panel members' rankings, once it was established that I was above the median, it didn't matter for the overall ranking whether my ranking was 3 or 20. If instead the mean had been the criterion, then that would have moved this solution up somewhat in the overall ranking.) By way of background, one-third of the world's population, 2.5 billion, does not have access to basic sanitation, and one billion defecate in the open. Improved sanitation could prevent 1.5 million deaths a year from diarrheal illness, enhance dignity, privacy, and safety, especially for women and girls. Modern water indoor sanitation systems cost $50-$100 per month, putting this technology out of reach for those living on, say, $1-2 per day. Conventional water waste treatment plants are expensive to construct and operate. One must look to latrines and septic tanks, investments for which the homeowner shoulders the responsibility of cost and maintenance. Developed nations use vacuum trucks for full septic tanks, but these trucks are expensive and not well suited for latrines. It is estimated that 200 million latrines and septic tanks are emptied manually, with a worker descending into the pit with a bucket and spade.

The "Sanitation as a Business" solution proposes a service provided by entrepreneurs at a cost of no more than $10 per household per year. It consists of emptying sludge to a treatment plant and treating it to acceptable levels before dispersal into the environment. Assume it is feasible to invest in innovation to achieve the following: bring annual cost of vacuum truck down from $35-90 to $20 as a result of more efficient markets, bring it down further to $10 with improved technology that is currently in design state. As subsidies necessary for introduction of the services, one is looking at a $320 million investment for improving service for 200 million people in low-income urban areas, giving a B/C ratio of 46:1. Assuming technological advancement doesn't pan out, so that it costs $20 per year instead of $10, then the B/C ratio falls to 23:1. Even under that more conservative estimate, this strikes me as an eminently worthwhile solution.

The area of sanitation has received a welcome burst of visibility lately with the news of the engagement of the Gates Foundation. In particular, as reported by The Economist, Bill Gates will provide seed money for the reinvention of the toilet in an attempt to make it cost-effective in low-income countries. Of course, one of the solutions considered by our panel was "The Reinvented Toilet," ranked #14 by me and #24 overall by the panel. But we were informed of Bill Gates' involvement, which suggests that, in spite of high potential B/C ratio (40:1, but with high risk), the involvement of CCC would not be crucial. Moreover, a factor, at least for me, is that it could take decades before this solution would be sufficiently cost effective to make inroads, for example as an alternative to "Sanitation as a Business."

Finn E. Kydland
October 2012

Individual ranking by Robert Mundell

	Solution
1	Bundled Micro-Nutrient Interventions
2	Deworming of Schoolchildren
3	Conditional Cash Transfers for School Attendance
4	Community Led Total Sanitation
5	Subsidy for Malaria Combination Treatment
6	Expanded Childhood Immunization Coverage
7	Investing in Effective Early Warning Systems
8	Increased Funding for Green Energy R&D
9	Expanding Tuberculosis Treatment
10	R&D to Increase Yield Enhancements
11	Salt Reduction Campaign
12	Community Walls Against Floods
13	Geo-Engineering R&D
14	Increase Availability of Family Planning
15	Accelerated HIV Vaccine R&D
16	Information Campaign on Benefits From Schooling
17	Hepatitis B Immunization
18	Heart Attack Risk Reduction Generic Pill
19	Extension of Protected Areas
20	Retrofitting Schools to Withstand Earthquake Damage
21	Acute Heart Attack Low-Cost Drugs
22	Strengthening Structures Against Hurricanes and Storms
23	Strengthening Surgical Capacity
24	Increasing Tobacco Taxation
25	Borehole and Public Hand Pump Intervention
26	Crop Advisory Text Messages
27	Sanitation as a Business
28	Protecting All Forests
29	Elevating Residential Structures to Avoid Flooding
30	The Reinvented Toilet

The modern world is subdivided into nation-states with governments that at best try to maximize the well-being of their constituents. The nation states typically have highly integrated economies while the WTO,

IMF, World Bank and as well as multilateral groupings of customs unions and free trade areas. There are also supranational entities like the UN and its subgroups that contribute importantly to such challenges as war, disease and poverty. But there is no world government or any other institution that specifically bridges the gap between global needs for public goods and global policies to close the gap.

The idea behind the Copenhagen Consensus—Bjørn Lomborg's idea—was to help bridge the gap by seeking out the "challenges" for global public spending and trying to determine the proportions of a given public sector budget that should be devoted to each challenge. A core panel of high profile economists, including many Nobel Laureates, would make the final evaluations. The challenges settled on for study were in ten major fields: armed conflict, chronic diseases, education, infectious diseases, population growth, biodiversity, climate change, hunger and malnutrition, natural disasters, and water and sanitation. The idea was to prepare studies in these fields by experts and then have them discussed with a core group of five high profile economists

The next step was to divide these broad categories into sub-groups associated with specific proposals. For example, the category of "infectious diseases" was sub-divided into four specific policies: A subsidy for Malaria Combination Treatment; expanded Childhood Immunization Coverage; Deworming of schoolchildren; and expanding Tuberculosis Treatment. Challenge papers—it turned out there were 39 such papers—were commissioned from acknowledged authorities in each field of policy and discussed at length with the core panel. There were also 14 "Perspective Papers" providing critical appraisals of each Challenge Paper's assumptions and methodology. Based on the costs and benefits of the solutions the panel ranked the proposals in descending order of desirability.

Another issue was the size of the budget. We economists were asked specifically how we would allocate $75 billion over four years to each production. That raised the question of how are choices would be affected by scale. The size of the budget is important for the results. $75 billion over four years would be just a drop in the bucket for some high-profile public projects (e.g., lowering global temperatures by control of hydrocarbon emissions).

In general, the rate of return on any investment or project depends on scale. The rate of return might for a time increase with scale as economies of coordination come into play (e.g., two men can lift a rock but not one). Eventually, increased investment will lead to a decline in the rate of return because of diminishing returns and limited absorptive capacity. We therefore allocated our budget of $18.75 billion per year (for four years) in a precise way such that at the levels of spending chosen resulted in equal rates of return. Thus one of the largest programs we chose was $3 billion to reduce under-nutrition for Pre-Schoolers but this does not mean that we valued this project more than the much smaller subsidies for malaria or accelerated HIV Vaccine R&D; it means instead that those levels of spending make the rates of return on the two projects the same.

I believe our panel did a good job in coping with the vast amount of information we had to absorb in the time available and I am happy to have been part of the project. Perhaps in the long run our contribution will point the way to a more sophisticated methodology for adjudicating global public policy projects that are crying out for attention.

Robert Mundell
October 2012

Individual ranking by Thomas Schelling

	Solution
1	Subsidy for Malaria Combination Treatment
2	Expanding Tuberculosis Treatment
3	Strengthening Surgical Capacity
4	Accelerated HIV Vaccine R&D
5	Expanded Childhood Immunization Coverage
6	Deworming of Schoolchildren
7	Bundled Micro-Nutrient Interventions
8	Salt Reduction Campaign
9	Increasing Tobacco Taxation
10	Acute Heart Attack Low-Cost Drugs
11	Hepatitis B Immunization
12	Conditional Cash Transfers for School Attendance
13	Borehole and Public Hand Pump Intervention
14	R&D to Increase Yield Enhancements
15	Geo-Engineering R&D
16	Investing in Effective Early Warning Systems
17	Increase Availability of Family Planning
18	Sanitation as a Business
19	Information Campaign on Benefits From Schooling
20	Increased Funding for Green Energy R&D
21	Heart Attack Risk Reduction Generic Pill
22	Crop Advisory Text Messages
23	Community Led Total Sanitation
24	Extension of Protected Areas
25	Protecting All Forests
26	Retrofitting Schools to Withstand Earthquake Damage
27	Elevating Residential Structures to Avoid Flooding
28	Community Walls Against Floods
29	Strengthening Structures Against Hurricanes and Storms
30	The Reinvented Toilet

I'm generally satisfied with the priority listing that I share with my colleagues. I have a few comments about the items above our "threshold" and one below.

"Conditional cash transfers for school attendance." This program is especially oriented toward girls. Earlier meetings of the Copenhagen Consensus have identified numerous valuable outcomes for girls. Examples are reduced teenage pregnancy, reduced risk of HIV infection, enhanced social valuation of women, improved health of newborn offspring, and of course greater participation in the labor force. There is experimental evidence, furthermore, that conditional cash transfers actually work: where they are available for either boys or girls, the main impact is increased schooling for girls. Cash transfers, thus, produce an important variety of benefits.

Geo-Engineering R&D reflects a recent coming-out-of-the-closet for a potential extremely effective and almost ridiculously economical climatic intervention the basis for which has been known for more than a hundred years, namely that certain particles introduced into the stratosphere that offset, by reflecting back into space about one or two percent of incoming sunlight, may offset the cooling effect of a doubling of the concentration of greenhouse gases in the earth's atmosphere. Mount Pinatubo in the Philippines erupted in 1991 and spewed thousands of tons of sulfur into the stratosphere, reducing the temperature of the surface oceans for a couple of years. What cannot be known without experiment—on a small scale at first, too small to affect climate—is what the possible dangers are, what the different regional impacts will be, and whether the results may be exceedingly disadvantageous for some parts of the world. Our intention is not to promote the deployment of such measures, but to find out more about them. If Geo-Engineering of that kind is a bad idea, the sooner we find out the better. If there are alternative substances that may work in the stratosphere, knowing which ones are most favorable would be important if ever there were an agreed need to proceed. This kind of intervention does not wholly solve the "greenhouse problem," continued growth of greenhouse gases in the atmosphere leads, among other problems, to increasing acidity of the ocean, which is deleterious to all marine animals that require calcium absorption for the production of their shells.

I believe that both the improving incomes in the developing world (so that men can afford tobacco), and the gradual emancipation of women from social norms against female smoking, are leading to an "epidemic" of an addictive habit that is gradually being brought under control in much of the developed world. One of the proposals under chronic diseases was for increasing tobacco taxation. We have not included that proposal, I believe, not because we oppose it but because there are no identifiable costs in increasing tobacco taxes for which it makes sense offer aid.

In earlier Copenhagen Consensus programs we had separate proposals for delivering vitamin A, iodine, iron, and a variety of other "micronutrients" that are cheap to purchase but sometimes expensive to deliver, there not being a suitable established infrastructure for that purpose in many developing nations. Because the "delivery" of these cheap but vital nutrients is the same for most of them, we have in this Consensus exercise "bundled" them, thereby reducing the cost of delivery. Somewhat the same may prove feasible for the delivery of deworming pills and perhaps of some vaccines. This anticipated lowering of costs of delivery helps to account for the high ranking enjoyed by the "bundling" of those interventions.

Strengthening of surgical capacity may sound ambitious, but what is proposed is actually providing assistance, such as for simple injuries like fractures or childbirth problems, that require not highly specialized surgeons but general practitioners and trained assisting staff that can deal with a multitude of ailments that can be seriously debilitating or fatal but that can be dealt with fairly inexpensively. This is essentially a form of "infrastructure" to support a wide range of surgical benefits that are frequently unavailable or inaccessible.

Accelerated HIV vaccine R&D yields by far the most delayed benefits of any of our selected projects. Its success is uncertain; success, if it happens, will be years away, perhaps decades; and the benefits will be distributed over its own future through the reduced transmission of HIV over the succeeding decades. We were persuaded that our modest budget for HIV vaccine development, on top of the larger ongoing investment, made sense.

Thomas Schelling
May 2012

Individual ranking by Vernon Smith

	Solution
1	Bundled Micro-Nutrient Interventions
2	Subsidy for Malaria Combination Treatment
3	Expanded Childhood Immunization Coverage
4	Conditional Cash Transfers for School Attendance
5	R&D to Increase Yield Enhancements
6	Deworming of Schoolchildren
7	Hepatitis B Immunization
8	Expanding Tuberculosis Treatment
9	Salt Reduction Campaign
10	Information Campaign on Benefits From Schooling
11	Protecting All Forests
12	Geo-Engineering R&D
13	The Reinvented Toilet
14	Increasing Tobacco Taxation
15	Borehole and Public Hand Pump Intervention
16	Strengthening Surgical Capacity
17	Heart Attack Risk Reduction Generic Pill
18	Investing in Effective Early Warning Systems
19	Community Walls Against Floods
20	Acute Heart Attack Low-Cost Drugs
21	Strengthening Structures Against Hurricanes and Storms
22	Accelerated HIV Vaccine R&D
23	Sanitation as a Business
24	Increased Funding for Green Energy R&D
25	Community Led Total Sanitation
26	Extension of Protected Areas
27	Retrofitting Schools to Withstand Earthquake Damage
28	Increase Availability of Family Planning
29	Elevating Residential Structures to Avoid Flooding
30	Crop Advisory Text Messages

The key contribution of the Copenhagen Consensus (CC) meetings is to draw attention to a particular way of thinking about world problems that is not part of the mainstream political and media debate. The question is not whether a particular policy is likely be beneficial, and command popular agreement; rather how does it stack up in comparison with the truly large and mind-boggling number of critical issues that might be on the table. These problems range from poverty to climate change, but each general topic contains a host of specific issues. The core idea in CC is that we cannot do everything. This implies the need for a mechanism that allows specific proposals to be prioritized. A useful mechanism for focusing the mind on this task is to suppose that one has a limited budget, and the objective is to get the most out of the available resources, in this case $75 billion over the next four years. In my view this is not intended as a central planner's exercise, but rather is directed to issues designed to sharpen the precision and centrality of that debate.

Toward that end, my prioritization reflects an attempt to answer the question: How to prioritize particular proposals to advance betterment in the quality of human life? For me, in this regard, our most pressing and continuing task is to deal with the ancient and continuing problem poverty. Moreover, surely there must be substantial agreement that the most effective means of reducing poverty is through mechanisms that better enable people to help themselves. Such programs are not only essential to individual self-fulfillment and actualization, but are also ultimately self-financing, perpetuating desirable outcomes without continued maintenance from external resources, enabling such resources to continue to be made available for other challenges.

Consequently, my top-ten list includes all the most promising, generally least uncertain, programs to alleviate life-long suffering and improve life-long performance in children: interventions that focus on the nearly 180 million children whose biological and mental development and maturation is stunted by under nutrition; childhood immunization; deworming of school children; and two programs designed to foster additional childhood years spent in school, investments that have a huge return that is especially large for girls. Once children are stunted, they become less reachable via and investment programs.

The other five programs in my top ten include: malaria treatment; R&D to enhance crop yields; Hepatitis B immunization; tuberculosis treatment; and salt reduction. Enhancing crop yields has well-proven claims of direct human benefit in avoiding mass starvation. Increasing crop yields also creates a direct bonus in climate benefits—an excellent example of doing good while doing well. Moreover, because of well-developed markets in agricultural commodity outputs and their inputs, basic new research findings in yield enhancement are likely to be properly calculated, evaluated and efficiently implemented via a private sector response to any new discoveries.

My next-ten list largely overlaps that of the consensus rankings of other panel members. I will use my limited space to discuss only one exception: I rated "Increase Availability of Family Planning" near the bottom. This challenge might seem on first blush to be particularly deserving of high priority as a means to increasing human betterment and personal choice freedom; however, I found the Lam (2012) perspective paper very persuasive in raising issues new to me, and effectively showcasing important weaknesses in the objective of isolating and estimating the benefits of extending family planning in regions with high fertility rates.

Kohler's (2012) challenge paper provides a well-documented summary of the impressive 50-year history across a multiplicity of cultural groups—with the exception of Sub Saharan Africa—attesting to decreases in the fertility rate as a historically common response to rising income and family economic betterment. Parents want fewer children, and to invest more in each child's preparation for life as they emerge from poverty. One's intuition is that surely this must mean that there is an important independent influence of birth control information provided by family planning programs.

As it turns out, evidence in support of this intuition is not that easy to demonstrate. The direct and most convincing evidence is in the Matlab program in Bangladesh (Joshi and Schultz 2007) and the family planning program in Colombia (Miller 2010) that have provided direct experimental measures of the direct effects of these programs on fertility, and indirectly on outcomes in health and education. As noted in the perspective paper, the critical link is the extent to which "…it is lack of access to family planning services that explains why some women who want no more children are not using contraception (Lam, 2012, p 2, Figure 1). If this link is weak, the benefit relative to cost of family planning is correspondingly diminished, and may pale in comparison with other Challenges. The many reasons women list for not using contraception imply that the availability of information is trumped by other considerations that are neither easily nor non-invasively changed by well-intentioned planning programs, i.e., additional contraceptive information is ineffective, whatever its potential benefits.

Turning to the Columbia experiments, Lam (2012, p 4) notes that "…the impact of Colombia's large family planning program was relatively modest, leading to a decline in fertility of about 1/3 of a child…in fertility over the 1964–93 period…The point is that estimates of unmet need and the cost of meeting that unmet need would almost surely lead to substantial overestimates of the actual impact of expanding family planning on fertility."

For future reference, a valuation issue that I have not been able to resolve deserves to be mentioned in this reflection. Kohler (2012, p 39) identifies an important benefit from Family Planning: Reduced Expenditures on Health and Schooling. Yet health and schooling in both the CC 2008 and CC 2012 are ranked very high in terms of their yield on investment. Hence, some fraction of the children not born, fail to benefit from these high yield investments, and to this extent are not a benefit but a cost of not being born; i.e., children are an intermediate input in these calculations. My point is that these interactions need to be taken into account, and spotlight the huge challenge in evaluating Family Planning as a desirable social expenditure.

Returning to the main theme, since the critical area of fertility concern is Sub-Saharan Africa, I could support a more limited program that would finance field experiments designed to measure the specific effects of birth control information on fertility in this region. The connection between information and realized fertility reduction would be the target of this exercise to be undertaken before embarking on a costly expansion of family planning programs into high fertility regions. It seems likely that this causal relationship will interact with cultural norms, and indeed these considerations may help to account for the stubborn resistance of fertility to meaningful declines in the region. In the meantime, I believe the resources are more efficaciously devoted to health and education investments, and other CC Challenges in the top-ten rankings.

Vernon L. Smith
May 2012

Individual ranking by Nancy Stokey

	Solution
1	Bundled Micro-Nutrient Interventions
2	Subsidy for Malaria Combination Treatment
3	Geo-Engineering R&D
4	Expanded Childhood Immunization Coverage
5	Investing in Effective Early Warning Systems
6	Expanding Tuberculosis Treatment
7	Acute Heart Attack Low-Cost Drugs
8	Deworming of Schoolchildren
9	Hepatitis B Immunization
10	Strengthening Surgical Capacity
11	R&D to Increase Yield Enhancements
12	Increased Funding for Green Energy R&D
13	Accelerated HIV Vaccine R&D
14	Heart Attack Risk Reduction Generic Pill
15	Community Led Total Sanitation
16	Information Campaign on Benefits From Schooling
17	Increase Availability of Family Planning
18	Borehole and Public Hand Pump Intervention
19	Sanitation as a Business
20	Crop Advisory Text Messages
21	Conditional Cash Transfers for School Attendance
22	Increasing Tobacco Taxation
23	Salt Reduction Campaign
24	The Reinvented Toilet
25	Retrofitting Schools to Withstand Earthquake Damage
26	Community Walls Against Floods
27	Strengthening Structures Against Hurricanes and Storms
28	Extension of Protected Areas
29	Protecting All Forests
30	Elevating Residential Structures to Avoid Flooding

The Copenhagen Consensus 2012 ranking reaffirms many of the conclusions from CC 2004 and CC 2008, but it also offers a couple of new and noteworthy ideas: R&D in geo-engineering and an early warning system for storms, floods, and tsunamis. My remarks will first discuss these new ideas in detail, and then look more briefly at the rest.

Geo-Engineering R&D I regret not ranking the proposal for R&D in geo-engineering as #1. This project deserves to have a flag waved to draw attention to it.

The proposal is to conduct additional laboratory investigations, followed by field trials, of a system for solar radiation management (SRM). This proposal appeared in the CC 2009 project on Climate Change, where it was #1 in the overall group rankings.

Although geo-engineering sounds very high-tech and rather frightening, the main idea is in fact quite simple. It involves enhancing by a small amount an effect that occurs naturally, the reflection of sunlight before it reaches the surface of the earth. Both ordinary clouds in the lower atmosphere and aerosols in the upper atmosphere naturally reflect about 30% of the sunlight directed at the earth. Sunlight that is reflected does not warm, and slightly enhancing reflectivity, by 1-2%, can offset the additional warming produced by greenhouse gases.

Funding is requested here for R&D on a system that uses rockets to inject small amounts of sulfites into the upper atmosphere, mimicking the effect produce by a large volcanic eruption. (The 2009 proposal also included R&D on a system that uses a flotilla of small, unmanned marine vessels, churning up seawater to "whiten" marine clouds.)

The total cost of the R&D proposed here is estimated to be about $500 million over 10 years. The cost in the early years, which involve mostly laboratory experiments, is tiny: $5 million. The annual costs rise to $30 million and then $100 million for the field trials later in the 10-year window. To be conservative, the authors multiply all of these costs by 10.

We face enormous uncertainty about climate sensitivity—about the stability of ice shelves in the Antarctic, about methane gas in the Arctic tundra, about the rate at which glaciers will melt, about snowpack in the Himalayas. As Bickel and Lane point out, "SRM is the only technology that could quickly cool the Earth should the need arise to do so."

It is impossible to assess the expected benefits of a program like this one with any accuracy. The chance that it will need to be deployed in the next century may be small, how small? Is the chance 0.1% or 0.01%? Or is it 1.0%? The benefit in case the need arises are similarly difficult to quantify. Is it $0.1 trillion or $1 trillion or $10 trillion? The system to be investigated offers at least some insurance against a catastrophe, at very low cost. And as Tom Schelling pointed out in the discussion, if there are any as-yet-unknown reasons not to deploy SRM, we should find out now.

Investing in Effective Early Warning Systems The second noteworthy addition is the proposal to provide upgraded hydro-meteorological services in developing countries. An early warning system for storms, floods, and tsunamis would save both lives and property. The proposed system would use information from existing earth observation satellites and global weather forecasts, so the required investment consists of local infrastructure to assess risks and communicate warnings. For high-risk areas, investments of this type look very attractive.

Health, Nutrition, Sanitation Infectious Disease and Chronic Disease are separate categories in CC2012, and these two categories, together with Hunger, took many of the top positions. The Expert Panel in 2012 unanimously agreed, as did the panels in 2004 and 2008, that health and nutrition programs offer extremely attractive opportunities for improving the lives of people in low-income parts of the world. As in the developed world, early childhood interventions are particularly effective, and many of these interventions are directed at young children.

Micro-nutrients (vitamin A, iodine, iron, zinc) got the top spot, this time in the form of a bundled package for infants under two years that also includes deworming and a highly nutritious peanut paste. Deworming appears again as a treatment for schoolchildren, who would probably benefit from the micro-nutrients as well. These interventions are directed at reducing infant mortality, preventing physical and cognitive stunting, and—for the older group—raising school attendance. These seem to be little or no question that these programs are feasible and that they are extremely cheap for the benefits they produce. Since early childhood begins in utero, pregnant women should also be a target group for these programs.

The Subsidy for Malaria Combination Treatment is a program designed by a blue-ribbon commission of economists and health experts to deal with the problem of drug-resistance in the malaria parasite. The typical treatment for malaria in many low-income countries consists of a single inexpensive drug. While the treatment is cheap and often effective, it has the unfortunate side-effect of promoting drug-resistant strains of the malaria parasite. The proposed intervention offers a subsidy to pharmaceutical companies, so they can sell a more expensive treatment that combines several drugs, at a similar low price. Artemisinin based combinations (ACTs) are more effective in treating malaria, and are in addition expected to reduce drug resistence. Thus, encouraging individuals to shift to ACTs is expected to produce global benefits by reducing child deaths, reducing transmission rates from infected individuals, and preventing the emergence of drug resistant strains. The program would also undermine the growing supply of "fake" ACTs.

Expanded Childhood Immunization and Hepatitis B Immunization also got very high ranks. The former can reduce child mortality rates at very low cost, while the latter bears life-long benefits in terms of reduced morbidity from illness.

Several other health proposals were also very promising: Expanding Tuberculosis Treatment, Acute Heart Attack Low-Cost Drugs, and Strengthening Surgical Capacity. The last involves training doctors or other medical personnel in existing health clinics to perform simple surgical procedures liked Caesarian sections. Subsidizing the provision of generic pills to reduce the risk of heart attack is not a bad idea, but does seem more costly relative to its benefits.

Two of the Water and Sanitation proposals are also health related. Standpipes and latrines are old ideas, here offered with some new twists. Community-Led Total Sanitation proposes updated latrines, with an eye to insuring that they are actually used. The proposal for Boreholes and Public Hand Pumps involves chlorinating water at the public source. This seems like a good idea, but other parts of the challenge paper sent a somewhat mixed message, noting that hand pumps often deteriorate and become inoperable after a few years.

Education, Population Growth There is an ongoing debate in the aid/development literature about the reluctance of individuals in low-income countries to make use of schools and family planning services. The debate revolves around whether the problem is supply (schools charge fees, family planning clinics are too far away) or demand (skepticism about the value of an education, religious or other objections to contraception).

The Education proposals for Information on Returns and Conditional Cash Transfers are attempts to work on the demand side. The former has been tried in only a couple of field experiments. The results are promising enough to make further trials worthwhile, although not to support a broad expansion on this front. The latter has been tried in a number of countries, and it seems to work, at least by the metric of better school attendance. The evidence for improved cognitive development or higher earnings after school completion is less solid, however. In addition programs of this type are expensive unless they are re-packaging existing transfers, so that only the 'conditionality' is an incremental cost.

The proposal to Increase Availability of Family Planning is an attempt to work on the supply side. The author defines "unmet need" as the number of women who are sexually active, who say that they do not want to become pregnant, and who nevertheless use no form of contraception. As one of the perspective paper points out, however, in the few areas where information is available, the "unmet need" seems to be less a supply issue than a demand issue. If this is so, simply increasing the availability of family planning clinics is probably not enough. Here, too, carefully planned field trials could be quite useful in determining what works. Until there is better evidence, a large investment is unwarranted.

Research & Development Proposals were offered for funding R&D in a number of other areas, in addition to geo-engineering. Specifically, there were projects for R&D in yield enhancements, in a vaccine for HIV/AIDS, in green technologies, in non-piped technologies for waste removal in urban areas (Sanitation as a Business), and in a reinvented toilet.

Investment in yield enhancement has a long track record and, consequently, a fairly predictable payoff. The right question about further investment here is probably the extent to which public funds are needed, and how much can be left to the private sector.

For the other R&D projects, the Expert Panel was offered little evidence to evaluate the expected return from additional funding. What particular green technologies would be investigated? Which aspects of waste removal require basic research? Is there a large portfolio of ideas for an HIV/AIDS vaccine that currently lack funding?

Not worth funding/inappropriate Crop Advisory Text Messages have been useful in some areas, providing farmers with information about the weather or about market prices for particular commodities. Cheap cell phones are widely available in the developing world, so large investments are not required to provide this kind of service. What is required is specialized local knowledge about what information is relevant. Private markets seem better suited to providing this kind of service.

Higher taxes on tobacco would surely reduce its consumption, and low-income individuals would be especially responsive to a large price increase. But taxing tobacco does not require any outside resources. On the contrary, such a tax would raise revenue. Nor does it require any particular expertise to levy an excise tax on tobacco. A government anywhere can do this on its own, if it feels that the health costs of tobacco are a high priority issue.

In the U.S., about 70 million adults suffer from high blood pressure. About 50% control it with medication—most of which are inexpensive generics, and a much smaller fraction control it with diet. With this evidence as background, it is not at all clear that Salt Reduction Campaigns in the developing world are a worthwhile investment.

The Reinvented Toilet, a machine that will—almost magically—deal with human waste without using water or sewer systems, is a dream for the future. Maybe it will happen, someday, but it is not a high priority for investment today.

Retrofitting Schools to Withstand Earthquake Damage, building Community Walls Against Floods, Strengthening Structures Against Hurricanes and Elevating Residential Structures are extremely expensive interventions, especially on the broad scale proposed here. At best, they would need to be targeted to regions with the highest risk. And the Community Walls have another drawback as well. With sea levels rising, how high should these walls be? Encouraging people to move to at-risk areas, by creating a false sense of security, could easily backfire.

Extension of Protected Areas and Protecting All Forests are ideas that sound nice, but on closer inspection look impractical.

The Challenge Paper on Armed Conflicts, while admirable in many respects, did not offer a concrete proposal for an intervention. Syria? Sudan? Somalia? And what should be done? The panel could not rank these proposals.

Carbon taxes Several proposals for carbon taxes were offered, but the panel chose—wisely—not to rank any of them. Our task was to allocate a (notional) budget of $75 billion over a four-year horizon. Two features make a carbon tax an unsuitable candidate for this exercise. First, as noted above, taxes require no funding. Indeed, a tax generates revenue. In addition, a carbon tax is a long-run policy and needs to be planned for decades or centuries, not four years.

Nevertheless, taxes on carbon dioxide and other greenhouse gases are, in the end, the only serious way to deal with the problem of climate change. The geo-engineering ideas described above are short-run tools, useful for dealing with possible crises or for buying time while green technologies come on line. At some point, however, we will have to stop relying on fossil fuels, and the only way that will happen is with a carbon tax.

A public commitment to such a tax, on a wide scale and with a rate that increases over time, is needed to provide the private sector with strong signals about the expected future returns from investment in such technologies. To be sure, there is a role for public investment in basic science in the relevant areas, but private funds will necessarily provide the bulk of the investment.

Reducing barriers to international trade was taken off the table for CC 2012 not because it is a bad idea. On the contrary, it is an outstanding idea. But, like taxing greenhouse gases, reducing trade barriers requires no funding. It is a matter of political will, not lack of funds to invest. Negotiating trade reforms has been a painfully slow process, and negotiating a carbon tax will be, if anything, more difficult. The time to start is now.

Nancy Stokey
May 2012

APPENDIX

Excerpts of Research Papers

EDUCATION

Excerpt of Research Paper by Peter F. Orazem

Now that most children in developing countries enroll in school, economic development strategies have shifted to enhancing their learning while in school. This has led to a focus on improvements in school quality. While such improvements should increase lifetime returns to schooling in like fashion to improvements in child health, investments in school quality have some important disadvantages to health interventions in a benefit/cost sense. On the cost side, these interventions are typically more expensive per recipient than are nutrition supplements or preventive health. On the benefit side, the link between investment and resulting human capital acquisition is weaker than that between treatment and desired health outcome. Our knowledge of which inputs generate quality schooling outcomes is very weak, and additional investments in school inputs are unlikely to generate the desired learning response. There is widespread acknowledgement that resources are used inefficiently, but efforts to improve resource management by devolving authority to local jurisdictions are as likely to fail as succeed. There is ample evidence of shirking by government teachers but efforts to increase monitoring have been disappointing. Use of alternative teachers, whether contract teachers or tutors, are often successful, but their use begs the question of why they must be hired when civil service teachers appear to be underperforming. In addition, if these teachers will be converted into permanent government employees eventually, we must presume that the benefits of using contract teachers or tutors will be fleeting. Tying teacher bonus payments to student performance on exams shows some promise, but there are too few studies to justify firm support for that option. Increasing years of schooling simply by providing accurate information on the returns to schooling is also quite promising and an inexpensive intervention, but again there are too few studies upon which to base a world strategy.

The most consistent evidence of success from schooling interventions in recent years comes from transfer payments targeted to the poorest segments of society conditional on the children attending school. These programs have consistently increased child attendance, even when the transfer is of modest size. Program administration costs have been lower than those of other social interventions. In addition to the positive schooling outcomes, these transfers have lowered the poverty rate, improved the nutritional status of poor households, and have increased the fraction of children receiving vaccinations and other health services. Even the most expensive and comprehensive of these programs, the Mexican PROGRESA/Oportunidades program, have met the benefit/cost criteria. Because the programs increase the intensity of child investment in school as well as increasing child time in school, they help to break the cycle of poverty whereby poor parents underinvest in their children's schooling and doom their children to poverty as well. And by increasing child attendance, we should see a concomitant increase in teacher attendance which will increase the quality of schooling offered to the poorest children in the country.

Nevertheless, these programs can only succeed in relatively developed countries where government institutions necessary to identify the poorest households, manage a large transfer program, and monitor child attendance are well developed. That would suggest the prospects for using conditional cash transfers would be best in countries in South or East Asia or in the more advanced countries of Africa. Caldès, Coady and Malluccio (2006) report that the per child cost of three conditional transfer programs in Latin America ranged from $468 to $514 in 2012 dollars. At $468/child, using conditional transfers for the poorest decile of all the children in South Asia would cost $7.8 billion, while targeting 10% of the children in East Asia would cost $6.7 billion. As a particular example, the annual cost of a conditional transfer program would be $320 million/year in Vietnam and $221 million in Thailand.

In the poorer countries, programs aimed at improving nutrient health of children are less expensive and can meet benefit/cost criteria despite the lower potential returns to human capital in such countries. Such programs can target very young children, taking advantage of potential increasing returns from interventions that bump up the marginal benefit from schooling. One could address the needs of all 175 million malnourished children in the developing world under age 6 at a cost of

1.1 Benefit/cost ratios from various interventions affecting schooling

	Low Discount (3%)			High Discount (5%)		
	Benefit	**Cost**	**BCR**	**Benefit**	**Cost**	**BCR**
Health and Nutrition Programs						
Bolivia preschool (Behrman et al, 2004)	$5,107	$1,394	**3.7**	$3,230	$1,301	**2.5**
Kenya worms (Miguel and Kremer, 2004)	$1,560	$3.5	**445.7**	$646	$3.5	**184.6**
Kenya preschool (Vermeersch and Kremer, 2005)	$1,560	$29.1	**53.6**	$646	$28.6	**22.6**
Iron supplements (Knowles and Behrman, 2005)	$474	$10.5	**45.1**	$330	$10.3	**32.0**
India worms (Bobonis et al, 2006)	$2,201	$112.0	**19.7**	$868	$112.0	**7.8**
Guatemala (Damon and Glewwe, 2009)	$622	$52	**12.0**	$301	$51	**5.9**
Information on Returns						
Madagascar (Nguyen, 2008)	$3,349	$2.30	**1456**	$1,455	$2.30	**632.6**
Dominican Republic (Jensen, 2010)	$7734	$417	**18.6**	$3356	$417	**8.1**
Conditional Cash Transfers						
Mexico (Behrman et al , 2011)	$2,679	$500	**5.4**	$1,082	$390	**2.8**
Nicaragua (Maluccio, 2009)	$6,003	$1,574	**3.8**	$4,412	$1574	**2.8**
Honduras (Glewe et al, 2004)	$9,178	$266	**34.5**	$4,064	$219	**18.6**
Colombia (Attanasio et al, 2005)						
Urban ages 8-13	$9395	$1,916	**4.9**	$3168	$1898	**1.7**
Urban ages14-17	$9395	$767	**12.2**	$5,957	$759	**7.8**
Rural ages 8-13	$9395	$767	**12.2**	$3168	$759	**4.2**
Rural ages14-17	$9395	$479	**19.6**	$5,957	$474	**12.6**
Ecuador (Schady et al, 2008)	$9100	$572	**15.9**	$4665	$572	**8.2**
Chile (Galasso, 2011)						
Urban ages6-15	0-21504[a]	$542	**0-39.7[a]**	0-9903[a]	$446	**0-22.2[a]**
Rural ages6-15	0[a]	$542	**0.0**	0[a]	$446	**0.0**
Cambodia (Filmer and Schady, 2009)	$1,849	$709	**2.6**	$939	$709	**1.3**

Notes: Costs are the present value of inducing one additional year of schooling. Benefits are the present value from an additional year of schooling evaluated over a 40 year work career, evaluated at the average annual wage in the country

Estimated impact of schooling was not significantly different form zero in some specifications. Estimates in rural areas were insignificant or negative.

roughly $5 billion per year using estimates provided by John Hoddinott and Mark Rosegrant in their challenge paper.

All countries could benefit from improved information on the true returns from schooling. Although only two studies have buttressed that recommendation, the costs are very low and the potential benefits are quite promising. If one used the Madagascar estimates of 8 cents per child (Nguyen, 2008), one could address all 670 million school aged children for $54 million, which is just implausibly low. However, there is certainly a case for applying the strategy in more piloted cases with rigorous evaluations so that we can get a better grasp of how best to transfer information on the benefits of schooling to children and their parents. The cost of a few more studies would be modest, and we would be ready to scale up four years from now once broader evidence is available.

ARMED CONFLICTS

Excerpt of Research Paper by J. Paul Dunne

Conflict is a major problem for the world and one that impacts most upon the very poorest individuals in the world. It has potentially huge costs which are generally never fully measured. The direct costs are always very evident in the headlines, but the indirect and legacy costs are much less apparent. It is possible to measure both direct and indirect costs, using accounting and counterfactual methods. Such studies find conflicts can be devastating in a number of ways, can have high economic costs, can have high spillover effects and are a major concern for development. Arguments remain that we may be interpreting the role of conflicts wrongly (Cramer, 2006) and that they can play a positive role, representing primitive accumulation, allowing the removal fetters on forces production, or making important institutional changes. But given the damage they can do the main focus is on their costs.

What is being measured by studies of the cost of conflict is unlikely to be the full legacy costs and there always remain the questions of what peace is and when does a conflict end. The high costs and complexity make the creation of solutions very difficult, but in some ways it is better to see the solutions as part of a process to deal with then problems at particular stages, rather than simple remedies. For this reason we put together a combination of instruments that are relevant for conflict prevention, intervention and then post conflict reconstruction.

In this paper an attempt has been made to estimate the likely costs and benefits of using new funds to contribute to each of the solutions, which as they are essential phases show a degree of overlap. The analysis starts by considering the solutions presented in Collier et al (2008), using estimates that still seem reasonable for the valuations involved and adjusting where necessary. The approach taken here is quite different and the instruments focused upon deal with differently. Each of the solutions contains a number of instruments and trying to determine what the cost of these is, does illustrate the issues involved. The results of the reasoning and calculations provide the estimates below:

2.1 Conflict prevention, benefits and costs (billion US$) and benefit/cost ratios

Solution	Assumptions	Benefits	Costs	Benefit Cost Ratio
Prevention	$1000 DALY, 3%	852	56	15.2
	$1000 DALY, 5%	606	54	11.2
	$5000 DALY, 3%	966	56	17.3
	$5000 DALY, 5%	726	54	13.4

Note: this assumes prevention averts three out of four conflicts and so 75% of the full four year costs

2.2 Conflict intervention, benefits and costs (billion US$) and benefit/cost ratios

Solution	Assumptions	Benefits	Costs	Benefit Cost Ratio
Intervention	$1000 DALY, 3%	852	100	6.4
	$1000 DALY, 5%	606	96	4.8
	$5000 DALY, 3%	966	100	7.2
	$5000 DALY, 5%	726	96	5.7

Note: This assumes that intervention averts 75% of the costs of conflict, as conflicts have already started.

2.3 Post conflict reconstruction, benefits and costs (billion US$) and benefit/cost ratios

Solution	Assumptions	Benefits	Costs	Benefit Cost Ratio
Post conflict	$1000 DALY, 3%	568	145	3.9
	$1000 DALY, 5%	404	138	2.9
	$5000 DALY, 3%	644	145	4.9
	$5000 DALY, 5%	484	138	3.5

Note: This assumes that post conflict reconstruction averts 50% of the costs of conflict, as the conflicts have already ended or are close to it.

Clearly the results suggest that most cost effective way of dealing with the cost of conflict is to prevent the conflicts taking place, although care needs to be taken that this is not being undertaken against the interests of the citizens of the countries –in some cases conflict may have positive outcomes. If conflicts do break out then the next stage is possible intervention. This is shown to be extremely cost effective, but again there are a number of political issues and some clear guidelines and procedures need to be agreed and there needs to be transparency. If intervention succeeds it will lead to the post conflict reconstruction phase earlier than it would have happened otherwise and the costs to the country and the international community are likely to be smaller. When conflicts do end what is needed for reconstruction is contingent on the nature of the conflict and the way it ended. Already considerable effort is made on post conflict reconstruction, but it can be more effective. Particularly important are the legacy costs of the conflict, such as more general violence within the society and these are usually not picked up. Post conflict policies can be costly but also are cost effective in preventing suffering, important externalities and building up economies that provide new markets and raw materials. While post conflict policies may not have the highest benefit costs ratio, they do represent necessities and already command the attention and resources of the international community.

It is important to emphasize that even with the efforts we have made the true costs of armed conflicts are still likely to be hugely underestimated. The unmeasureables are significant and the full legacy costs are not always registered as the cost of the conflict. The existence of drugs, criminal gangs and violence in South American countries such as Colombia in the present day, can be traced back to the ending of an armed conflict without true peace being achieved.

The solutions here have fitted the costs into the 4 year window specified for the project, but clearly it would make sense to continue these expenditures. The benefits reflect the long run impact of the expenditures, but might be greater if a longer time frame was used. It may be possible to have some immediate impacts in prevention and intervention, but the post conflict reconstruction initiatives are for the long run and in the past have failed because of short run attitudes. Prevention and intervention have received not nearly enough attention and more research is certainly required to provide consistent and comprehensive cost benefit analyses of these potential solutions to conflict.

The bottom line is that without peace there cannot be development and the Millennium goals and other development targets become unattainable. So one might see the contributions to the solutions discussed here as necessities, to create an environment where the other challenges can be hope to be attained. If this is accepted the benefits we have calculated here can only been seen as a mere fraction of what could be achieved.

CLIMATE CHANGE

This challenge paper consists of four separate contributions, updating key research papers from the Copenhagen Consensus on Climate Change project from 2009.

An Updated Analysis of Carbon Dioxide Emission Abatement as a Response to Climate Change

Richard S. J. Tol

A Technology-led Climate Policy in a Changing Landscape

Isabel Galiana

Christopher Green

Market and Policy Driven Adaptation

Francesco Bosello

Carlo Carraro

Enrica De Cian

Climate Change: Climate Engineering Research

J. Eric Bickel

Lee Lane

AN UPDATED ANALYSIS OF CARBON DIOXIDE EMISSION ABATEMENT AS A RESPONSE TO CLIMATE CHANGE

Excerpt of Research Paper by Richard S. J. Tol

In the Copenhagen Consensus for Climate 2010 (Lomborg 2010), reduction of carbon dioxide emissions received a low priority. This follows from the particularities of the *Gedankenexperiment* that is at the core of all Copenhagen Consensus: There is a finite budget, that needs to be spent, on a separate project, informed by disjoint cost/benefit analyses.

Climate policy does not fit in that mould, and carbon dioxide emission reduction fits least.

Climate change is a big problem. In order to halt anthropogenic climate change, the atmospheric concentrations of greenhouse gases need to be stabilized. For that, carbon dioxide emissions need to be reduced to zero. This requires a complete overhaul of the energy sector. That is a big job. It should be done as long as the benefits exceed the costs. If it does not fit in the budget of the Copenhagen Consensus, then more money should be raised. Indeed, it would be profitable to borrow money if the benefit/cost ratio is greater than one.

There is wide agreement in the economic literature that greenhouse gas emission reduction is best done through a carbon tax. A uniform carbon tax implies equimarginal abatement costs. Climate change is a stock problem, so a price instrument is more robust to uncertainty than a quantity instrument. Taxes properly incentivise R&D. That is, climate policy is not about spending money. It is about raising money (and, of course, about finding the best way to spend the revenues raised through a carbon tax.)

3.1.1 Selected characteristics of the scenarios: Initial carbon tax, peak year of carbon dioxide emissions, atmospheric concentration of carbon dioxide in 2100, net present value of the costs of emission reduction, benefit/cost ratio

Scenario	Tax	Peak year	Concentration	NPV costs	Benefit/cost ratio
7	$1.8/tC	2090	875	$70 10^9	1.56
5	$2/tC	2090	850	$100 10^9	1.51
6	$3/tC	2080	815	$280 10^9	1.02
4	$12/tC	2055	675	$2,000 10^9	0.26
3	$250/tC	2010	425	$47,600 10^9	0.02

Drastic reduction of carbon dioxide emissions would be very expensive with current technologies. R&D is a critical part of CO_2 abatement policy. However, most of that R&D is innovation and diffusion, rather than invention. Grants are suitable for invention. For innovation and diffusion, the regulator should create a credible promise of a future market: In this case, the promise of an emission reduction target or, better, a carbon tax in the future. The best way to give a credible signal is to start now – which has an additional advantage because the regulator does not know how close to market renewable energy technologies really are. That is, R&D and CO_2 abatement are complements, not substitutes.

Cost/benefit analysis, the purported aim of the Copenhagen Consensus, is an analysis of efficiency. Cost-efficacy is a pre-condition for efficiency. Cost-efficacy requires that all alternative solutions to a problem – carbon dioxide emission reduction, reduction of other greenhouse gases, carbon capture and storage, and indeed R&D and geoengineering – are priced equally at the appropriate margin. It is inconceivable that a cost/benefit analysis would conclude that climate change is a problem that should be addressed through one channel – say geoengineering – but not through other channels, provided that those channels are complements and their marginal cost curves go through the origin.

Geoengineering indeed is a complement to carbon dioxide emission reduction. Geoengineering addresses warming, a subset of climate change, whereas carbon dioxide emission reduction addresses the whole of climate change as well as ocean acidification. Geoengineering is a transient, end-of-pipe solution to climate change whereas carbon dioxide emission reduction is a permanent, structural solution. Geo-engineering may have a place in an optimal portfolio of climate policy because carbon dioxide emission reduction will take considerable time to sort an effect, but it cannot dominate the portfolio.

The Copenhagen Consensus for Climate 2010 overlooks these issues. Its conclusions are therefore unsupported.

A TECHNOLOGY-LED CLIMATE POLICY IN A CHANGING LANDSCAPE

Excerpt of Research Paper by
Isabel Galiana and Christopher Green

In 2009 we proposed a technology-led climate policy (Galiana and Green 2009). Specifically, we proposed that on average $100 billion be spent globally on basic research and development, testing and demonstration of low carbon energy technologies plus required infrastructure support. The expenditure would be supported by a low carbon tax (we suggested $5.00/t$CO_2$) the revenues from which would be placed in dedicated trust funds in each participating country. Over time the carbon price would rise gradually (we suggested a doubling every 10 years) thereby sending a forward price signal to commercialize and deploy scalable, cost-effective energy technologies as they became available.

There are several reasons for proposing a technology-led climate policy. Five stand out, and each was elaborated on in some depth in Galiana and Green (2010). First we demonstrated that the size of the energy technology challenge to "stabilizing climate" is huge, and that it has been seriously understated by those who use the IPCC emission scenarios as baselines for estimating the size and cost of that challenge. Second, we examined the low carbon energy sources and found a current lack of technological readiness and scalability. Third, we explained why we cannot depend on carbon pricing to generate the needed long term investments in *basic* research and development the fruits of which may not prove successful; and if successful may take decades rather than years to prove so; and even then may generate benefits that are not appropriable. Fourth, we showed that a "brute force" approach to reducing GHG emissions in the absence of technological readiness could generate economic costs an order of magnitude or more, greater than the GDP cost estimates presented by the IPCC. Finally, we calculated that an effective technology-led policy would pass a benefit/cost test by wide margins.

In this paper an attempt has been made to update of our proposal. Is it as compelling as it was three years ago? Would it continue to pass a benefit cost test with high marks? Is there anything important that has changed or has occurred that should be considered in a reevaluation of the proposal? Our answers to the three questions are: *yes* to compelling; *still high* to benefit/cost test; and *yes indeed* to whether the landscape has changed and there is new information to consider. It is the last of these that is the chief focus of the update.

3.2.1 DICE model results from 2009 CC on CC (3% discount rate)

	Early return to R&D	Mid return to R&D	Late return to R&D
2010-2110	3.64	3.31	2.23
2010-2200	11.66	10.95	8.59

CLIMATE ENGINEERING R&D

Excerpt of Research Paper by
J. Eric Bickel and Lee Lane

With the results of detailed analysis of benefits and costs found in the in-depth Challenge paper, we present the estimates of the BCR (benefit-cost ratio) of SRM R&D. We define the BCR of R&D as

$$BCR = \frac{\text{Present Value of Net Benefits}}{\text{Present Value of R\&D Expenditures}}$$

Assuming that an SRM R&D program would require a total investment of $5 billion, as we detailed in the full paper, we obtain the BCR estimates shown in the following table.

3.3.1 BCR of SRM R&D under No Controls and Emissions Controls:

	SRM Damages			
	0%	1%	2%	3%
NC SRM2C	2,107	1,497	877	247
EC SRM2C	1,844	1,530	1,214	895

Thus, we believe the BCR for SRM R&D is large: possibly between about 250 and 2000 to 1. The actual BCR depends up the damages caused by SRM. As a rough estimate, though, we might say the BCR is 1000 to 1. Again these results assume that an SRM R&D program would be successful. But the very large net benefits that would flow from the success of SRM argue that R&D is a very good investment. Even a 10% chance of success will result in an expected-BCR of 100 to 1.

Climate Engineering R&D: Why Not?

If one believes that climate change will result in significant damages either due the warming itself or the costs imposed by abatement measures, then the ability to reduce warming at low cost will accrue substantial benefits. Given that the technology to achieve these benefits does not exist and might itself cause damage, research is likely to pay large dividends.

We believe the analysis outlined in this paper makes a compelling case for climate engineering research. Why then do some oppose it? What is the case against research? There are five primary arguments:

1. The climate system's complexity is beyond our capacity to understand and therefore any intervention is fraught with risk and should be considered unsafe (Cicerone 2006).

2. SRM will be perceived as a substitute for greenhouse gas controls and therefore society will lose its will to implement emission controls (Cicerone 2006).

3. Some environmentalists object to SRM on the grounds that it treats the symptoms of manmade climate change rather than removing its root cause (Tetlock and Oppenheimer 2008).

4. The development of technology to reduce warming may trigger international tensions and even conflict as countries vie for the right to choose the optimal climate (Victor 2009).

5. SRM is inherently unjust because (1) its benefits and costs will not be uniform, (2) it places future generations at risk, and (3) it is inexpensive and thus could be implemented unilaterally (Svoboda 2011).

6. Once started, it might be stopped prematurely resulting in rapid warming and increased damages (Goes et al. 2010).

Addressing all of these concerns in detail is beyond the scope of our current effort, however, we would like to offer a few thoughts, which we number in accordance to the list above.

1. Complexity. First, complexity of the climate system also makes it difficult to know the degree to which increased GHG concentrations will cause harmful climate change. Second, ignorance is in any case an argument for research rather than one against it.

2. Substitution. One might argue that SRM should only be deployed as a "last resort." While this is easy to say and might allow one to discuss SRM without controversy, we do not subscribe to this view. First, how do we define "last resort"? Even if the answer were clear, will we be able to tell that such a moment has arisen? Second, it may indeed be economic to replace some degree of emissions reductions with SRM. Substitution might well lessen both climate damages and the costs of GHG controls. We are not aware of any proof that such a blended strategy is clearly suboptimal. What valid reason, then, could warrant suppressing a welfare enhancing policy option, and, absent an order of Platonic guardians, on what authority would it be done?

3. Treating symptoms. This approach is often the most cost-effective available response: "Typically in an attempt to find a solution to a problem people look to its causes, or yet more fatuously, to its root causes. However, there need be no logical connection between the cause of a problem and appropriate or even feasible solutions" (Collier 2010). Thus, in economics, medicine, and politics treating symptoms often lowers total costs. The high institutional hurdles to curbing greenhouse gas emissions suggest that, with climate change too, treating symptoms may offer great benefits.

4. Conflict. Except for purely domestic adaptation, all steps to cope with climate change are likely to trigger some level of conflict. Efforts to control emissions certainly have. Growing global interdependence strengthens all states' incentives to cooperate. Yet the interests of major states often conflict. States build regimes such as the World Trade Organization to lower the transaction costs of cooperating on the issues on which they have some interests in common and some in conflict. (Keohane 1984). Experienced diplomats expect that were SRM to be deployed, the major powers would form a regime to govern its use (Benedick 2011).

5. Justice. No action we may take in response to climate change will result in uniform costs/benefits and remove all risk from future generations. In fact, a failure to research and deploy SRM would be unjust by this standard because it moves future generations towards a climate tipping point.

6. Termination. For two reasons, once SRM starts, there will be strong incentives to continue it. First, termination would be unlikely just because it would be costly. Second, as interest groups organize around existing programs, government policy often develops strong path dependence. Further, the validity of the case against a start and stop use of SRM depends heavily on what will happen if SRM is not used. Bickel and Agrawal (2011) detail many cases where SRM would produce net benefits even if it was aborted.

In sum, SRM is a family of technologies that could offer immense benefits. The proposed research program is inexpensive, a small fraction of current climate science R&D spending and the CC12 budget. The time has come to begin researching this approach to dealing with climate change.

CLIMATE CHANGE ADAPTATION

Excerpt of Research Paper by
Francesco Bosello, Carlo Carraro, and Enrica De Cian

This paper addresses the question of how resources for climate change should be allocated between adaptation, mitigation, and residual damage from climate change. The study adopts a macro-angle and uses the AD-WITCH model, an Integrated Assessment Model (IAM) that has been developed for the joint analysis of adaptation and mitigation.[1] With respect to the existing studies in the field (de Bruin et al., Hof et al., 2009; Hof et al., 2010; Bosello et al., 2010b, Bahn et al., 2010) the proposed modeling framework provides a novel characterization of the adaptation process, which includes not only anticipatory and reactive adaptation, but also adaptation specific technological change. This enables us to:

1. Analyse adaptation to climate change both in isolation and jointly with mitigation strategies
2. Provide a comparative cost/benefit analysis of both adaptation and mitigation
3. Assess the marginal contribution to the benefit/cost ratio of different adaptation modes
4. Emphasise region-specific characteristics of climate policy

The study is organised as follows. First we present a cost/benefit analysis of macro, policy-driven responses to climate change, namely, adaptation, mitigation, and joint adaptation and mitigation. By narrowing down the focus on policy-driven adaptation, we will then compute the benefit/cost ratios of three macro adaptation strategies (reactive, anticipatory or proactive, and knowledge adaptation).

---

[1] The model has been developed by FEEM in cooperation with the OECD team led by Shardul Agrawala.

A second novel contribution of this work is the assessment of the market potential to adjust to climate change and to reduce the vulnerability of economic systems to climate change. To some extent, adaptation will occur without any policy intervention, as a reactive response to changes in climate, driven by market price signals. Although market-driven adaptation has a strong damage smoothing potential at the global level, we show that damages are likely to remain significant, especially in developing countries. We therefore compute and discuss the benefit/cost ratios of different policy-driven adaptation strategies net of market-driven, autonomous adaptation to climate change.

AD-WITCH, the model used to carry out most of the analysis, is an optimal growth Integrated Assessment model endowed with an adaptation module to compute the costs and benefits of policy-driven mitigation and adaptation strategies. Given the game-theoretic and regional structure of AD-WITCH (see Bosello et al 2010a), both first best and second best climate policies can be computed. In this study, we focus on a first best world in which all externalities are internalized. The social planner implements the optimal levels of adaptation and mitigation, namely the level that equalizes marginal costs and benefits.

To account for both market-driven and policy-driven adaptation, two different modeling tools have been used. The ICES model, which is a highly disaggregated computable general equilibrium model, has been used to identify the effects of market–driven adaptation. ICES and AD-WITCH have then been integrated to provide a full assessment of both market- and policy-driven adaptation. More precisely, the effects of market-driven adaptation on regional climate damages have been estimated using the ICES model. These estimates have been used to modify all regional climate change damage functions in the WITCH model to compute climate damages net of market-driven adaptation.

The final part of this study describes specific adaptation proposals. These are consistent with the analysis carried out in the first part of the study, and build upon existing estimates of costs and benefits of specific adaptation strategies.

3.4.1 Benefit/Cost Ratio (BCR) of adaptation and of joint adaptation mitigation

Discounted values over the period 2010-2105	BCR adaptation		BCR joint adaptation and mitigation
	Non cooperative	Cooperative	Cooperative
Benefits	16	14	19
Costs	10	8	9
BCR	1.67	1.73	2.11

Note: Benefits are measured as discounted avoided damages compared to non-cooperative no policy case

Adaptation costs are measured as discounted expenditures on adaptation

Mitigation costs are measured as additional investments in carbon-free technologies and energy efficiency compared to the non-cooperative no policy case

3.4.2 Sensitivity analysis. Benefit/Cost Ratio (BCR) of adaptation and of joint adaptation and mitigation in the cooperative scenario

Adaptation

Discounted values over the period 2010-2105	LDAM_HDR	HDAM_HDR	LDAM_LDR	HDAM_LDR
Benefits	14	55	99	337
Costs	8	21	65	144
BCR	1.73	2.63	1.52	2.33

Joint adaptation and mitigation

Discounted values over the period 2010-2105	LDAM_HDR	HDAM_HDR	LDAM_LDR	HDAM_LDR
Benefits	19	67	294	811
Costs	10	24	266	347
BCR	1.93	2.82	1.10	2.34

Values are discounted using a 3% discount rate the LDAM_HDR and HDAM_HDR cases and 0.1% discount rate in the LDAM_LDR and HDAM_LDR cases.

3.4.3 Benefit/Cost Ratio (BCR) of adaptation strategy mix in the cooperative scenario

Option excluded from the optimal mix

Discounted values over the period 2010-2105	Reactive Adaptation	Anticipatory Adaptation	Knowledge Adaptation
Benefits	789	7.4	13657
Costs	771	5.7	7938
BCR	1.02	1.30	1.72

3.4.4 Sensitivity analysis. Benefit/Cost Ratio of adaptation and of joint adaptation and mitigation in the cooperative scenario – OECD regions

Adaptation

Discounted values over the period 2010-2105	LDAM_HDR	HDAM_HDR	LDAM_LDR	HDAM_LDR
Benefits	2.2	16	14	93
Costs	1.5	5.9	12	39
BCR	1.45	2,64	1.12	2.38

Joint adaptation and mitigation

Discounted values over the period 2010-2105	LDAM_HDR	HDAM_HDR	LDAM_LDR	HDAM_LDR
Benefits	4.2	21	68	238
Costs	1.8	6.6	146	164
BCR	2.23	3.17	0.46	1.45

Values are discounted using a 3% discount rate the LDAM_HDR and HDAM_HDR cases and 0.1% discount rate in the LDAM_LDR and HDAM_LDR cases.

3.4.5 Sensitivity analysis. Benefit/Cost Ratio of adaptation and of joint adaptation and mitigation in the cooperative scenario – NON-OECD regions

Adaptation				
Discounted values over the period 2010-2105	LDAM_HDR	HDAM_HDR	LDAM_LDR	HDAM_LDR
Benefits	11	40	86	243
Costs	6	15	53	105
BCR	1.79	2.63	1,61	2,31

Joint adaptation and mitigation				
Discounted values over the period 2010-2105	LDAM_HDR	HDAM_HDR	LDAM_LDR	HDAM_LDR
Benefits	15	46	226	573
Costs	6.9	16	128	183
BCR	2.11	2.85	1.77	3.13

Values are discounted using a 3% discount rate the LDAM_HDR and HDAM_HDR cases and 0.1% discount rate in the LDAM_LDR and HDAM_LDR cases.

3.4.6 Benefit/Cost Ratio (BCR) of policy driven adaptation in the presence of market driven adaptation

with Market-driven adaptation			
Discounted values over the period 2010-2105 (US$ 2005 Billion)	WORLD	OECD	NON OECD
Benefits	5282	202	5079
Costs	3123	164	2959
BCR	1.69	1.24	1.72

w/o Market-driven adaptation			
Discounted values over the period 2010-2105 (US$ 2005 Trillion)	WORLD	OECD	NON OECD
Benefits	14	2.2	11.5
Costs	8	1.5	6.4
BCR	1.73	1.45	1.79

BIODIVERSITY

Excerpt of Research Paper by
S. Hussain, A. Markandya, L. Brander,
A. McVittie, R. de Groot, O. Vardakoulias,
A. Wagtendonk, and P. Verburg

This paper has analysed the challenge of ecosystems and biodiversity. Under business as usual there will be a significant loss of biodiversity over the next 40 years: our estimates indicate that globally it could be around 12 percent, with South Asia facing a loss of around 30 percent and Sub-Saharan Africa of 18 percent. These losses have a significant value, based on the services that the different biomes provide. These include timber and other forest products, genetic materials, recreational and cultural uses of the biomes, non-use values and carbon values. They have been estimated in monetary terms in a number of studies for the three main biomes (temperate and tropical forests, and grasslands), using a meta-analysis linking the unit values of the services in each biome to the characteristics of the particular patch of biome over which the estimates were made. From this meta-analysis we derive figures for the losses that will occur when any patch of the same biome is lost. This approach is applied to all biomes and ecosystem services except for carbon values which are based on a review of the literature. For the carbon values a range is taken, with the lower bound based on marginal damage studies and an upper bound based on the marginal costs of abatement arising from a target of a 50 percent global reduction in emissions by 2050.

The study looked at three interventions relative to the business as usual. The first was an increase in agricultural productivity (20 percent for crops and 40 percent for livestock), which reduces pressure on land. The benefit cost ratios for this program were very favourable: with a total cost over the period 2000 to 2050 of US$373 billion at a 3% discount rate the non-carbon benefits alone were well in excess of that. If we take the carbon benefits valued using the MD (the lower of the two unit values) the ratio goes to 7.5 at a 3% discount rate and around 6 at a discount rate of 5%. Hence we would argue that there is a strong case for such a program.

4.1 Overall benefit/cost ratios for agricultural productivity (2000 to 2050)

	Discount rate	3%	5%
Benefits of change in biome areas (bn US$2007)		1,631	960
Carbon values (bn US$2007)			
	POLES	6,019	3,166
	RICE-Mean	1,182	720
Costs (bn US$2007)		373	265
Benefit/cost ratios			
No carbon value		4.4	3.6
Carbon value Based on MAC (POLES)		20.5	15.6
Carbon value based on MD (Rice-Mean)		7.5	6.3

The second program was to increase the amount of protected areas globally to around 20 percent of all land across a large number of ecological regions. Currently such areas account for around 10 percent of all land. There are obvious benefits from this but there are also significant costs, principally the loss of output from the land taken out of use. The net benefits are very much dependent on what cost estimates are taken as valid. With these figures set at the best guess, the program was just beneficial with the lower of the carbon values. If, however, the costs were at the upper end, the program did not have a benefit cost ratio of more than one even with higher carbon values. This suggests that only a selective increase in protected areas is warranted – in situations where the opportunity costs are low and the ecosystem services gained are high.

A further comment about protected areas is warranted. The main reason for these programmes is really to enhance biodiversity conservation and our methods of estimation do not fully capture those benefits. Hence the assessment made here underestimates the benefits of such policies.

4.2 Overall benefit/cost ratios for protected areas

	Discount rate	3%	5%
Benefits of change in biome areas (bn US$2007)		299	211
Carbon values (bn US$2007)			
	POLES	132	70
	RICE-Mean	63	39
Costs (bn US$2007)		373	265
	'Best guess'	305	239
	Upper	1,305	1,024
Benefit/cost ratios			
No carbon value	'Best guess'	1.0	0.9
	Upper	0.2	0.2
Carbon value based on MAC (POLES)	'Best guess'	1.4	1.2
	Upper	0.3	0.3
Carbon Value based on MD (Rice-Mean)	'Best guess'	1.2	1.0
	Upper	0.3	0.2

The final program was one that sought to prevent all dense forests from conversion. In this case the benefits are very high and while there is considerable uncertainty about the costs (the upper bound is more than four times the lower bound) the benefit cost ratio exceeds one even with the higher cost figures and without the carbon values. When the carbon values were included the ratio went well above one, indicating that such a program would be very attractive.

The Challenge specifies that the amount available is around US$75 billion per year for four years. The amounts involved in these programs are in excess of that figure but there are spread out over a longer period as well: over 50 years in the case of the first intervention and over 30 years in the case of protected areas and reduced deforestation. The detailed analysis did not indicate that there was any notable non-linearity in the programs; in other words the benefit/cost ratios should not be significantly different if the programs were conducted at a fraction of the scale considered here. In fact one could argue that a smaller program could have a higher benefit to cost ratio if one could pick out the areas where it was applied so as to keep the costs lower and the benefits higher. This should certainly be possible in the case of the reduced deforestation option, although perhaps less so to the increasing agricultural productivity option. In any event these two options could easily share the budget of US$75 billion over four years (possibly spending it over a longer period) and generate benefits that would result in benefit cost ratios similar to the ones reported here. One caveat we have add is that these programs cannot be readily aggregated. Consequently there is likely to be significant double counting if the programs are combined, i.e., changes in land cover for any one patch may apply over more than one program, e.g. any given patch of forest might not be converted to pasture under high AKST and would not be converted to another use under reduced deforestation.

4.3 Overall benefit/cost ratios for reduced deforestation (REDD)

	Discount rate	3%	5%
Benefits of change in biome areas (bn US$2007)		1,590	1,121
Carbon values (bn US$2007)			
	POLES	3,522	2,408
	RICE-Mean	1,866	1,369
Costs (bn US$2007)		373	265
	'Best guess'	163	127
	Upper	441	346
Benefit/cost ratios			
No carbon value	Lower	9.8	8.8
	Upper	3.6	3.2
Carbon value based on MAC (POLES)	Lower	31.3	27.8
	Upper	11.6	10.2
Carbon Value based on MD (Rice-Mean)	Lower	21.2	19.6
	Upper	7.8	7.2

One final remark about the methodology that merits consideration is the fact that it is based on a partial equilibrium analysis. That is to say, changes in biomes are valued on the assumption that the amounts involved are small compared to the total size of the biome and the services it provides. If that assumption is not valid then the estimates of changes will be flawed to the extent that other prices, as well as unit values of the services themselves may change. We have been at pains to note the size of the change in biomes and services are relatively small but that is a matter of judgment and in one or two cases the proposed measures may be considered as possibly non-marginal. In that case there may have been an overestimate of the benefits.

NATURAL DISASTERS

Excerpt of Research Paper by
Howard Kunreuther and Erwann Michel-Kerjan

During the past few years the world has experienced a series of truly devastating natural disasters that have taken many lives and triggered unprecedented economic losses. Hurricane Katrina in 2005 in the United States, the 2010 massive floods in Australia and the 2011 earthquake/tsunami in Japan have demonstrated that even the richest and most prepared countries in the world can experience large-scale damage and destruction. The situation is much worse in low-income countries since they often do not have the financial means to protect their population and economy against catastrophes, or do not consider it a priority. The earthquake in Haiti in 2010 illustrates the challenges of an unprepared and poor country.

Despite this upward trend, knowledge about exposure to natural disasters on an international scale is still rather limited. The recent development of probabilistic catastrophe models can be of significant help in this regard. This paper utilizes this methodology to undertake benefit/cost analyses (BCAs) for disaster-reduction measures by first focusing on a single building in the Caribbean (wind hazard from hurricanes), Indonesia (flood hazard) and Turkey (earthquake hazard).

5.1 Earthquake Risk in Istanbul:
B/C Ratios Taking into Account
the Value of Life for Baseline Type 1 and Measure 1
(Amounts greater than 1 in bold)

Analysis	Time Horizon (Years)	Camlibahce Min Hazard Discount Rate	
		5%	12%
Value of statistical life not included	10	0.12	0.09
	25	0.22	0.12
VoL= $750,000	10	0.7	0.5
	25	1.3	0.7
VoL= $6 million	10	4.5	3.5
	25	8.1	4.9

5.2 Proposal II (flood protection)
Discount rate of 3%; VoL: $40,000

Measure	Investment	Cumulative Benefit	Lives Saved	Average BCR	Countries which will benefit the most
Community-Wall	$75 billion	$4.5 trillion	19,894	**60.1**	Cambodia; Laos; Bhutan; Somalia; Central African Republic; Afghanistan; Myanmar; Bangladesh; Korea; Chad; Sudan; Viet Nam; India (partially)
Elevating houses	$75 billion	$1.1 trillion	7,195	**14.5**	Cambodia; Laos; Bhutan; Somalia; Central African Republic; Afghanistan; Myanmar; Bangladesh (partially)

5.3 Proposal III (Wind protection against hurricanes, cyclones and storms) – 3% discount rate

VoL	Investment	Benefit	BCR	Lives Saved
$6 million	$75bn	$354bn	**Average: 4.7** Min/Max: 2/18.6	60,761
$1.5 million	$75bn	$214bn	**Average: 2.8** Min/Max: 2/6.7	60,761
$200,000	$75bn	$173bn	**Average: 2.3** Min/Max 2/3.3	60,761
$40,000	$75bn	$168bn	**Average: 2.2** Min/Max: 2/2.9	60,761

Undertaking a similar benefit/cost analysis for the building portfolio of an entire country is a very time consuming and complex process. It requires a detailed knowledge of the hazard in different parts of the country (down to the local level) and the distribution and location of the entire building portfolio. This portfolio would comprise all residences, commercial and industrial construction, critical infrastructure, and all government buildings. Such detailed inventory is usually not available in low-income countries, so studies published in the literature have typically focused on one city or part of a community with respect to a specific hazard. A national risk assessment would require knowledge of the vulnerability of the entire portfolio of structures to all the hazards faced by the country. To undertake a BCA one would also need to determine for each loss reduction measures under study the cost of raw material and labor cost in different part of the country too.

For all those reasons, we have undertaken rather preliminary BCAs, building on limited studies that have been undertaken in different parts of the world to reduce losses from natural disasters. For three types of disasters — earthquakes, floods and cyclones/hurricanes/storms — we have focused on residences and schools in more than 30 countries each. We have determined the cost of different loss reduction measures and expected benefits in terms of physical damage reduction and number of lives saved. By design our BCAs are highly dependent on very simplifying assumptions we had to make. Furthermore, and as expected, the selection of different discount rates, time periods and values of life can have a significant impact on our findings.

Note, however, that our analysis has not taken into account several additional benefits from these disaster risk-reducing measures in the form of reduction of evacuation costs (from reducing housing damage), lowering the number of injured and possible subsequent health issues, continuity of education (from preserving schools) and relieving social stress to individuals and avoiding business interruption (Heinz Center, 2000).

We also discussed the importance of behavioral and economic barriers to implementing measures even though they can appear to be cost effective on paper. Moreover, in addition to risk assessments and cost/benefit analyses of specific loss reduction measures, one needs to design strong risk financing mechanisms for victims of disasters (individuals and firms) to get back on their feet more quickly after a catastrophe rather than relying on uncertain donor's money. Insurance and other alternative risk transfer instruments can play an important role here. In addition there is a need for innovations with short-term incentives (such as multi-year contracts) that could be more attractive to those living and working in exposed areas as well as to politicians who are concerned with re-election or staying in power and could grasp the short-term benefits of such innovations.

POPULATION GROWTH

Excerpt of Research Paper by Hans-Peter Kohler

Combining the estimates presented in this project of the benefit/cost ratios for family planning programs in the area of reducing maternal/child mortality and increasing income per capita suggest benefit/cost ratios for investments in family planning programs of 90:1 to 150:1. Table 6.1 summarizes how these benefit/cost ratios arise from benefits in terms of reduced infant and maternal mortality and income growth. High and low estimates for the former are due to different evaluations of life, and in the latter, due to different costs of achieving a specific reduction in fertility and population growth rates.

6.1 Summary of costs, benefits and benefit/cost ratios for family planning programs Annual Net Benefits and Costs (3% discount rate)

Benefit Component:	Assumptions	Annual benefits Billion USD	Annual costs* Billion USD	BCR
Reduced Infant and Maternal Mortality	Low (DALY = 1K)	110	3.6	30
	High (DALY = 5K)	180		50
Income Growth (including life cycle, distributional and intergenerational benefits)	Low	216	3.6	60
	High	360		100
Total, Family Planning programs (sum)	Low	326	3.6	90
	High	470		150

*of satisfying unmet need in developing countries

In summary, therefore, the conclusion based on the review of the literature and assessment of benefit/cost ratios for the expansion of family planning programs is quite consistent with several related recent studies that have argued in favor of the expansion of family planning programs (Ashraf et al. 2008; Babigumira et al. 2012; Chao 2005; Cleland et al. 2006, 2012; Haveman 1976; Hubera and Harveya 1989; Joshi and Schultz 2007; Levine et al. 2006; Miller 2010; Simmons et al. 1991; US-AID Health Policy Initiative 2009b; Wulf 1981). Our discussion and benefit/cost analyses thus lend support to earlier analyses that have argued that family planning programs are a good "*economic investment*" (Bongaarts and Sinding 2011b) and the renewed emphasis on family planning programs in light of continued population growth in some of the world's least developed countries is very much supported by the present analyses. In expanding family planning programs, it is clear— and supported by a fairly broad consensus—that these programs must be voluntary and based on a long-term commitment of resources, and empirical studies suggest that, in order to be effective, family planning programs are ideally integrated with other reproductive and child health services, effective community-based programs and potentially related behavioral change communication. There is also a rich body of empirical evidence and experience that can inform the important open questions about the optimal design and implementation of these programs. And while the *Expert Panel* of the Copenhagen Consensus Project 2012 Copenhagen Consensus Project (2012) did not rank family planning programs particularly favorable in comparison with other proposed interventions for confronting ten great contemporary global challenges, the readers of the *Slate Magazine Forum* accompanying the Copenhagen Consensus 2012 Project ranked population growth and family planning as a top priority (Lomborg 2012a,b). Based on the evidence reviewed in this paper, this author tends to agree with the *Slate* readers. Indeed, as recently stated by Melinda Gates (2012b), "*Let's put birth control back on the agenda*".

WATER AND SANITATION

Excerpt of Research Paper by
Frank Rijsberman and Alix Peterson Zwane

Bill & Melinda Gates Foundation

This Challenge Paper focuses on sanitation, as the world has met the water Millennium Development Goal, but will likely miss the sanitation target. It considers what it would cost to improve service for both the unserved population in developing countries, those one billion or so who must defecate in the open, and what it would cost to improve the quality of service for those people in urban areas who are nominally "served" but struggle to realize the gains from sanitation because of the challenges of emptying and safely disposing of latrine/septic tank contents. Dramatically cutting open defecation rates in rural areas has been shown to be feasible with a reasonable public investment. At a scale of tens of millions of people, it has a positive, though modest, pay-off as measured by benefit cost analysis. Rural water interventions, which we consider briefly (as water was covered extensively in the previous Copenhagen Consensus round), have similar modest pay-offs. In the case of urban sanitation, the theoretical benefits of basic onsite sanitation will not be achieved unless specific innovations are put in place. Investments in technological and institutional innovations to reduce the cost and increase the effectiveness of sanitation services to empty and treat human waste collected in latrines and septic tanks would have a very large pay-off. We believe the innovation required is achievable and that there is credible evidence that the fraction of roll-out costs to achieve adoption that would need to be borne by the public sector is sufficiently small as to make such an investment feasible and attractive. Finally, there is also a need for radical innovation to "reinvent the toilet". Such radical innovation is indeed high risk, but if successful would lead to very attractive benefit cost ratios.

We have based the calculations in this paper largely on the extensive cost and benefit data published recently by the very significant Economics of Sanitation Initiative (ESI) of the Water and Sanitation Program of the World Bank, resulting from its research undertaken over 2007-2011 on the impacts of sanitation and the economic returns to sanitation interventions in over 20 Asian and African countries. The data this program has generated fill a real gap in knowledge concerning the costs and benefits of basic onsite non-networked sanitation as well as modern networked sewerage and treatment systems. We have generally accepted the cost data for wet and dry latrines in urban and rural areas as realistic and the best available. We have also accepted the benefit estimates of sanitation as the best available.

ESI concludes that basic sanitation, wet and dry latrines, have the highest Benefit Cost Ratios of all sanitation interventions, in a range of 5 to 8. We do not agree that current technology does indeed generate these benefits, both because the adoption rates for dry latrines are low in rural areas and the lack of effective and affordable latrine emptying and fecal sludge treatment services means that particularly in low income urban areas, the benefits estimated by ESI are not realized.

We propose three sanitation interventions that can potentially help realize the benefits estimated by ESI and have analyzed their Benefit Cost Ratios (BCR) as follows:

CLTS++, a behavior change program to create demand for sanitation in rural areas: an investment of US$3 billion could serve 600 million people, 50% of the rural population currently without basic service, with a BCR of 4-7 at a discount rate of 8%. This is a low-risk investment already demonstrated to be effective at a scale of tens of millions of people. Targeted subsidies for the poor will likely be a critical element of a successful program, so that Open Defecation Free status can be achieved and health gains realized.

Sanitation as a Business, latrine emptying and fecal sludge processing services at an annual cost of US$10 per household: an investment of US$320 million ($120 million in technology and institutional innovation, and a further $200M in market development) could serve 200 million low-income urban people, 20% of the latrines currently emptied manually, with a BCR of 23-47. This is a medium risk investment in a product and development innovation package, key elements of which have already been demonstrated to be feasible.

Reinvented Toilet, an off-the-grid toilet that processes and recycles human waste at household scale and provides an excellent user experience affordably: an investment of US$125M ($50M in technology innovation and product development, and a further $75M in market development) could serve a billion low income urban people, 100% of the latrines currently emptied manually (and potentially many more people) with a BCR of 40. This is a high-risk investment in research, product development and market development for a product currently at the proof-of-concept / prototype stage.

The fourth intervention we propose is based on the analysis presented in the Copenhagen Consensus paper of Whittington et al (2008), it is a rural water intervention which consists of boreholes equipped with handpumps. An investment of $12-23 billion could potentially reach some 700 million people with water services, with a BCR of around 3.4. This is a low-risk investment in proven solutions that are primarily in need of increased levels of resources to roll them out to unserved populations. These results are summarized below in table 7.1.

7.1 Summary of BCR analysis

Intervention	Investment (US$ M)	BCR	People served (M)	Risk
CLTS++	3,000	**4-7**	600	low
Sanitation as a Business	320	**23-47**	200	medium
Reinvented Toilet	125	**40**	1000	high
Rural Water	12,000-23,000	**3.4**	700	low

INFECTIOUS DISEASE

Excerpt of Research Paper by
Dean T. Jamison, Prabhat Jha, Ramanan Laxminarayan,
and Toby Ord

This paper identifies key priorities for the control of infectious disease, injury and reproductive health problems for the Copenhagen Consensus 2012 (CC12). It draws directly upon the disease control paper (Jamison, Bloom and Jha, 2008) from Copenhagen Consensus 2008 and the AIDS vaccine paper for the Copenhagen Consensus Rethink HIV project (Hecht and Jamison, 2011). This paper updates the evidence and adjusts the conclusions of the previous work in light of subsequent research and experience. For CC12 noncommunicable diseases (NCDs) are being treated in a separate paper (Jha, Nugent, Verguet, Bloom and Hum, 2012) that complements this one. This paper's conclusions emphasize investments in control of infection. That said, one of the six investment areas advanced – essential surgery – addresses both complications of childbirth and injury and points to the potential for substantial disease burden reduction in these domains. All these papers build on the results of the Disease Control Priorities Project (DCPP).[2] The DCPP engaged over 350 authors and estimated the cost-effectiveness of 315 interventions. These estimates vary a good deal in their thoroughness and in the extent to which they provide regionally-specific estimates of both cost and effectiveness. Taken as a whole, however, they represent a comprehensive canvas of disease control opportunities.[3] We will combine this body of knowledge with the results from research and operational experience in the subsequent four years.

---

[2] The DCPP was a joint effort, extending over 4 years, of the Fogarty International Center of the U.S. National Institutes of Health, the World Bank, and the World Health Organization with financial support from the Bill & Melinda Gates Foundation. While the views and conclusions expressed in this paper draw principally on the DCPP, others might draw different broad conclusions. In particular views expressed in this paper are not necessarily those of any of the sponsoring organizations.

[3] See Jamison et al (2006) and Laxminarayan et al (2006).

8.1 Disease Control: Investment Solutions

Solution	Indicative benefit/cost ratio	Level of capacity required	Financial Risk Protection Provided	Relevance for development assistance	Annual costs ($ billions)	Annual benefits
1. *Tuberculosis: appropriate case finding and treatment, including dealing with MDR TB*	**15:1**	M	H	M	1.5	1 million adult deaths averted or 30 million DALYs
2. *Malaria: subsidy for appropriate treatment via AMFm*	**35:1**	L	M	H	0.3	300,000 (mostly child) deaths averted or 10.5 million DALYs
3. *Childhood diseases: expanded immunization coverage*	**20:1**	L	L	L	1	1 million child deaths averted or 20 million DALYs
4. *HIV: accelerated vaccine development*	**11:1**	L	H	H	0.1	24% reduction in HIV incidence 15 years after introduction
5. *Essential surgery: to address difficult childbirth, trauma and other*	**10:1**	H	H	H	3	30 million DALYs
6. *Deworming schoolchildren*	**10:1**	L	L	L	0.3	About 300 million children dewormed

a This refers to level of capacity required for implementation in a developing country. While HIV vaccine development, for example, requires enormous scientific capacity, that capacity is functionary already where the development work would be undertaken.

The DCPP concluded that some interventions are clearly low priority. Others are worth doing but either address only a relatively small proportion of disease burden or simply prove less attractive than a few key interventions. This paper identifies 6 key interventions (TB treatment, Malaria, Childhood immunization, HIV, Injury and deworming) in terms of their cost-effectiveness, the size of the disease burden they address, the amount of financial protection they provide, their feasibility of implementation and their relevance for development assistance budgets. The resulting 'dashboard' of indicators underpins overall judgments of priority.

CHRONIC DISEASE

Excerpt of Research Paper by
Prabhat Jha, Rachel Nugent, Stéphane Verguet,
David Bloom, and Ryan Hum

Eighty percent of global deaths from heart disease, stroke, cancer, and other chronic diseases occur in low- and middle-income countries. This paper identifies priorities for control of these chronic diseases as an input into the Copenhagen Consensus effort for 2012 (CC12). The paper and the accompanying CC12 paper on infectious disease control build on the results of the CC 2008 paper on disease control (Jamison et al, 2008), and is best read as an extension of the CC08 paper on disease control.

This paper draws on the framework and findings of the Disease Control Priorities Project (DCP2).[4] The DCP2 engaged over 350 authors and among its outputs were estimates of the cost-effectiveness of 315 interventions including about 100 interventions for chronic diseases. These estimates vary a good deal in their thoroughness and in the extent to which they provide regionally specific estimates of both cost and effectiveness. Taken as a whole, however, they represent a comprehensive canvas of chronic disease control opportunities. This paper

---

[4] The DCP2 was a joint effort, extending over 4 years, of the Fogarty International Center of the U.S. National Institutes of Health, the World Bank, and the World Health Organization with financial support from the Bill & Melinda Gates Foundation. While the views and conclusions expressed in this paper draw principally on the DCP2, others might draw different broad conclusions. In particular views expressed in this paper are not necessarily those of any of the sponsoring organizations.

The DCP2 resulted in two main volumes, both of which Oxford University Press published in 2006. One book deals with the *Global Burden of Disease and Risk Factors* (Lopez et al., 2006). The other book, *Disease Control Priorities in Developing Countries, 2nd edition* (Jamison et al., 2006) discusses interventions to address diseases and risk factors and the health systems to deliver those interventions. A first edition was published by Oxford University Press for the World Bank in 1993. This paper will refer to these two volumes as *DCP1* and *DCP2*.

identifies 5 key priority interventions for chronic disease in developing countries which chiefly address heart attacks, strokes, cancer, immunization, and tobacco-related respiratory disease. These interventions are chosen from among many because of their cost-effectiveness, the size of the disease burden they address, their implementation ease and other criteria. Separate but related papers for CC 2008 deal with other major determinants of chronic diseases such as nutrition, (Behrman, Alderman and Hoddinott, 2008), air pollution (Larsen, Hutton, Khanna, 2008) and education (Orazem, 2008). The health related papers for CC12 are focusing on infectious diseases (Jamison et al, 2012), sanitation and water (Rijsberman and Zwane, 2012), education (Orazem, 2012), hunger and under nutrition (Hoddinott et al) and population growth (Kohler, 2012).

The main conclusions of this paper are several. First, chronic diseases already pose a substantial economic burden, and this burden will evolve into a staggering one over the next two decades. Second, although high-income countries currently bear the biggest economic burden of chronic diseases, countries in the developing world, especially middle-income, are expected to assume an increasing share as their economies and populations grow. Third, the marginal costs for governments of achieving maximal adult survival are rising, in contrast to declines in marginal costs of achieving child survival. This divergence is a consequence chiefly of the lack of tobacco control in most low- and middle-income countries, the lack of sustained investments in new drugs, and gaps in the strategies and in the program implementation for chronic diseases. This leads to the fourth conclusion, which is that addressing chronic disease in poor countries requires a concomitant rethinking of developmental assistance and possibly new delivery approaches. Finally, selected options available to prevent and control chronic diseases appear to justify themselves in economic terms in the sense that the welfare gains and the economic losses that could be averted by investments that would reduce chronic diseases are considerably larger than those investments.

9.1 Chronic disease control: key investment priorities

Priority Area	Indicative Benefit/cost Ratio	Level of Capacity Required[a]	Financial Risk Protection Provided[a]	Relevance for Development Assistance[a]	Annual Costs ($ billions)	Annual Benefits[b]
1. Cancer, heart disease, other: tobacco taxation	40:1	L	H	H	0.5	1 million deaths averted or 20 million DALYs
2. Heart attacks (AMI): acute management with low-cost drugs	25:1	H	H	H	0.2	300,000 heart attack deaths averted each year or 4.5 million DALYs
3. Heart disease, strokes: salt reduction	20:1	M	H	H	1	1.3 million deaths averted or 20 million DALYs
4. Hepatitis B immunization	10:1	H	H	H	0.1	150,000 deaths averted or 3 million DALYs
5. Heart attacks and strokes: secondary prevention with 3-4 drugs in a "generic risk pill"	4:1	H	H	H	32	1.6 million deaths averted or 118 million DALYs averted

[a] Level of capacity required, extent of financial risk protection provided and relevance for development assistance, are judged by the authors to be high (H), medium (M) or low (L).

[b] In the formulation of DALYs the benefits of averting a death in a given year all accrue in that year and are calculated as the present value (at a 3% discount rate) of the future stream of life years that would have occurred if the death had been prevented.

HUNGER AND MALNUTRITION

Excerpt of Research Paper by
John Hoddinott, Mark Rosegrant, and Maximo Torero

Current estimates suggest that there are approximately 925 million hungry people in the world. Just under 180 million pre-school children are stunted, that is they are the victims of chronic undernutrition. This deprivation is not because of insufficient food production. Approximately 2,100 kcals/person/day provides sufficient energy for most daily activities; current per capita global food production, at 2,796 kcal/person/day is well in excess of this requirement. Given that there is more than enough food in the world to feed its inhabitants, global hunger is not an insoluble problem.

Deprivation in a world of plenty is an intrinsic rationale for investments that reduce hunger and undernutrition, our focus in this paper, as with previous Copenhagen Consensus (CC) papers on this topic, Behrman, Alderman and Hoddinott (2004) and Horton, Alderman and Rivera (2008) is on the instrumental case for doing so. In its simplest form, the central argument of this paper is that these investments are simply good economics. Our solutions, however, represent a partial departure from those earlier CC papers. First, we re-introduce attention to solutions to hunger with a focus on investments that will increase global food production. This might seem strange given our observation that global food production exceeds global food needs. But as we argue, these investments are needed for two reasons: to lower prices so as to make food more affordable; and because given the consequences of climate change, there can be no complacency regarding global food production. Second, previous CC papers on hunger and undernutrition have considered very specific interventions that focus on single dimensions of undernutrition. In this paper, we examine the economic case for bundling these. Our proposed investments are:

- Investment 1 – Accelerating yield enhancements
- Investment 2 – Market innovations that reduce hunger
- Investment 3 – Interventions reduce the micronutrient malnutrition and reduce the prevalence of stunting

We begin with background material that contextualizes our proposed solutions: What are the causes of hunger? How many hungry and undernourished people are there in the world? And what are the likely trends in hunger over the next 25-35 years? We then describe our three proposed investments explaining how each addresses the problems of hunger and undernutrition and describing their costs and benefits. Caveats and cautions are noted in section 4 of the full version of the paper and our concluding section summarizes the case for these investments.

10.1 Benefit/cost ratios of investments that increase yields

	Discount rate		
	Three percent	Five percent	Ten percent
Benefits derived from yield enhancement (billion USD)	4561	2475	702
Cost (billion USD)	214	154	87
Benefit/cost ratio	21.31	16.07	8.07

10.2 Estimates of impacts and benefit/cost ratios of ICT intervention under different benefit and cost scenarios

	Bangladesh	India	Kenya	Ghana	Senegal	Tanzania
Scenario 1: Base benefits, base costs						
Increase in income (%)	2.40%	2.40%	3.75%	3.75%	3.75%	3.75%
Reduction in Poverty	1.9%	1.9%	2.3%	2.3%	2.3%	2.3%
Increase in income ($PPP)	6.53	7.14	8.31	8.23	6.47	5.62
Net benefit PC	2.55	3.16	4.33	4.25	2.49	1.64
Benefit/cost ratio	1.64	1.79	2.09	2.07	1.63	1.41
Scenario 2: Conservative benefits, base costs						
Increase in income (%)	1.0%	1.0%	2.0%	2.0%	2.0%	2.0%
Reduction in Poverty	0.8%	0.8%	1.2%	1.2%	1.2%	1.2%
Increase in income ($PPP)	2.72	2.98	4.43	4.39	3.45	3.00
Net benefit PC	-1.26	-1.00	0.45	0.41	-0.53	-0.99
Benefit/cost ratio	0.68	0.75	1.11	1.10	0.87	0.75
Scenario 3: High benefits, base costs						
Increase in income (%)	4.80%	4.80%	7.50%	7.50%	7.50%	7.50%
Reduction in Poverty	3.8%	3.8%	4.5%	4.5%	4.5%	4.5%
Increase in income ($PPP)	13.06	14.28	16.61	16.46	12.94	11.23
Net benefit PC	9.08	10.3	12.63	12.48	8.96	7.25
Benefit/cost ratio	3.28	3.59	4.17	4.14	3.25	2.82
Scenario 4: Base benefits, reduced costs						
Increase in income (%)	2.40%	2.40%	3.75%	3.75%	3.75%	3.75%
Reduction in Poverty	1.9%	1.9%	2.3%	2.3%	2.3%	2.3%
Increase in income ($PPP)	6.53	7.14	8.31	8.23	6.47	5.62
Net benefit PC	4.54	5.15	6.32	6.24	4.48	3.63
Benefit/cost ratio	3.28	3.59	4.18	4.14	3.25	2.82
Scenario 5: Conservative benefits, reduced costs						
Increase in income (%)	1%	1%	2%	2%	2%	2%
Reduction in Poverty	0.8%	0.8%	1.2%	1.2%	1.2%	1.2%
Increase in income ($PPP)	2.72	2.98	4.43	4.39	3.45	3.00
Net benefit PC	0.73	0.99	2.44	2.4	1.46	1.01
Benefit/cost ratio	1.37	1.50	2.23	2.21	1.73	1.51
Scenario 6: High benefits, reduced costs						
Increase in income (%)	4.80%	4.80%	7.50%	7.50%	7.50%	7.50%
Reduction in Poverty	3.8%	3.8%	4.5%	4.5%	4.5%	4.5%
Increase in income ($PPP)	13.06	14.28	16.61	16.46	12.94	11.23
Net benefit PC	11.07	12.29	14.62	14.47	10.95	9.24
Benefit/cost ratio	6.56	7.18	8.35	8.27	6.50	5.64

10.3 Benefit/cost ratios of micro-nutrient interventions

Micronutrient	Intervention	Previous Copenhagen Consensus Estimates		New estimates			Current estimates of cost per beneficiary
		BAH	HAR	Rajkumar et al (2012)	Horton et al (2011)	Other	
Iodine	Salt iodization	15-520	30	81			$0.05 (HAR)
Iodine and iron	Doubly fortified salt			2.5	2 - 5		$0.25 (Horton)
Iron	Supplements, mothers and children 6-24 months	82 -140		23.8			$0.96 (Rajkumar)
	Supplements, pregnant mothers			8.1			$2.00 (Horton 2010)
	Fortification, general		7.8			6.7	
	Fortification of wheat flour				9.1	(Casey, 2011)	$0.17 (Horton)
	Home fortification				37		$1.20 (Horton)
	Biofortification	11.6-19	16.7				< $0.01 (Horton)
Vitamin A	Supplement	4.3 - 43	6.1 -250	12.5			$0.29 (Rajkumar)
Zinc	Supplement			2.85			$1.26 (Rajkumar)

Source: Authors' compilation. BAH is Behrman, Alderman and Hoddinott (2004). HAR is Horton, Alderman and Rivera (2008).

10.4 Benefit/cost estimates of investments that reduce stunting

		23.8 percent income increase		15 percent income increase	
		Discount rate		Discount rate	
		5 percent	3 percent	5 percent	3 percent
Bangladesh	Increased income, NPV	3647	7165	2303	4523
	Cost	96.1	96.1	96.1	96.1
	Benefit/cost ratio	38.0	74.6	24.0	47.1
Ethiopia	Increased income, NPV	2289	4496	1445	2838
	Cost	96.1	96.1	96.1	96.1
	Benefit/cost ratio	23.8	46.8	15.0	29.5
Kenya	Increased income, NPV	3713	7295	2344	4605
	Cost	96.1	96.1	96.1	96.1
	Benefit/cost ratio	38.6	75.9	24.4	47.9
India	Increased income, NPV	7875	15470	4972	9767
	Cost	111.62	111.62	111.62	111.62
	Benefit/cost ratio	70.6	138.6	44.5	87.5

Source: Authors' calculations.

CORRUPTION AND POLICY REFORM

Excerpt of Research Paper by
Susan Rose-Ackerman and Rory Truex

Policies designed to improve the quality of life for the poor and to spur economic growth often fail. A program that succeeds in one country or even in one village may not work in another. Promising experiments may not be capable of replication and may be impossible to scale up to cover an entire country. Reformers are told: "One size does not fit all." Yet, problems of poor health, low educational attainment, degraded natural environments, and violence and crime are widespread. Why shouldn't similar policies work in various settings? We argue that, over and above substantive differences, a key reason for cross-country differences in policy efficacy is the quality of government and the ubiquity of corruption and related forms of self-dealing by politicians, civil servants, and the private individuals and business interests with whom they interact. A policy that works quite well in one country may fail or be coopted in another with lower quality governance.

Understanding the incentives for corruption and self-dealing is a precondition for making progress on the other challenges facing the world. A beautifully designed policy that seems to have high net benefits may fail in the face of weak institutions.[5] One response is to urge a crackdown by law enforcement authorities, but that strategy will seldom be sufficient. Those seeking to further economic development need to understand the institutional origins of corruption and take them in to account in designing polices. Certain policies may simply be infeasible because they are riddled with incentives for illicit self-dealing. Others may need to be combined with programs explicitly designed to reduce the incentives for corruption built into existing institutions.

---

[5] In an evaluation of a rice distribution program in Indonesia, Olken (2006) finds that around 18 percent of the rice was lost from the program due to corruption. Under reasonable assumptions, the welfare losses from the missing rice outweigh the redistributive gains.

To set the stage for our analysis, we are summarizing the macro-data on the overall costs of corruption and then review research that illustrated the specific mechanisms by which corruption lowers human welfare. Next, we explain how corrupt incentives arise in a variety of contexts. We outline the basic "corruption calculus" that underlies corrupt behavior. Understanding why people and businesses pay and accept bribes and engage in other forms of malfeasance is a necessary first step towards limiting the damage that corruption causes.

We then discuss six linked types of reforms that each can be part of an overall strategy. We discuss solutions that involve external monitoring and enforcement combined with the punishment of wrongdoers. Recognizing the limited impact of such strategies, we are concentrating on bottom-up reforms under which the victims of corruption help to limit its incidence. We discuss internal controls ranging from reforms in the civil service system to the redesign of programs and service delivery to limit the opportunities for illicit gains. We move to the top of the government hierarchy to discuss the control of high-level corruption that distorts infrastructure projects, defense spending, privatization of public assets, and concession contracts. We locate situations where the private market can substitute for the state to limit corrupt incentives. Even when such opportunities exist, however, the process of shifting assets or services from public to private ownership can itself be corrupted. Sometimes a fall in public corruption simply means a rise is private corruption. Finally, we discuss a set of new initiatives at the international level. We conclude with some reflections on the state of the art of quantitative research on corruption and its reform.

TRADE BARRIERS AND SUBSIDIES

Multilateral and Regional Reform Opportunities

Excerpt of Research Paper by
Kym Anderson

Numerous barriers to international trade in goods, in some services, and in capital flows have been reduced considerably over the past three decades. Even so, many remain. Such policies harm most the economies imposing them, but the worst of the merchandise barriers (in agriculture and textiles) are particularly harmful to the world's poorest people. This paper focuses on how costly those anti-poor trade policies are, and examines possible strategies to reduce remaining distortions. The opportunities addressed include completing the stalled Doha Development Agenda process at the World Trade Organization (WTO), and three different ways of freeing up trade in the biggest part of the world economy not yet covered by a comprehensive regional integration agreement, namely the Asia-Pacific region. A review of the economic benefits and adjustment costs associated with these opportunities provides the foundation for undertaking benefit/cost analysis, as required to rank these opportunities against those aimed at addressing the world's other key challenges identified by the Copenhagen Consensus project. The paper notes several analytical caveats before concluding that taking up these opportunities – especially the multilateral Doha Round – could generate huge global social benefit/cost ratios that are considerably higher than the direct economic ones quantified in this study. In addition, they could also contribute to alleviating several of the other challenges identified by the Copenhagen Consensus project, including malnutrition, disease, poor education and air pollution.

11.1 Benefit/cost ratios, from reducing trade barriers and subsidies globally under the WTO's Doha Development Agenda

	3% discount rate		5% discount rate	
	Low	High	Low	High
World	136	179	90	99
Developing countries	215	249	146	136

11.2 Benefit/cost ratios, from reducing trade barriers and subsidies under three alternative Asia-Pacific regional trade agreements

	3% discount rate			5% discount rate		
	TPP	ASEAN+3	FTAAP	TPP	ASEAN+3	FTAAP
World	65	89	174	38	54	95
Developing countries	121	133	216	65	75	110